THE SMITH MANOEUVRE

Is your mortgage tax deductible?

Fraser Smith

Trafford Publishing

National Library of Canada Cataloguing in Publication Data

Smith, Fraser, 1938-
The Smith manoeuvre / Fraser Smith.
ISBN 1-55369-641-7
1. Mortgage loans--Canada.
2. Income tax deductions for interest--Canada. I. Title.
HG2040.5.C2S62 2002 336.24'216 C2002-904141-4

TRAFFORD *Printed in Victoria, Canada*

This book was published *on-demand* in cooperation with Trafford Publishing.
On-demand publishing is a unique process and service of making a book available for retail sale to the public taking advantage of on-demand manufacturing and Internet marketing. **On-demand publishing** includes promotions, retail sales, manufacturing, order fulfilment, accounting and collecting royalties on behalf of the author.

Suite 6E, 2333 Government St., Victoria, B.C. V8T 4P4, CANADA
Phone 250-383-6864 Toll-free 1-888-232-4444 (Canada & US)
Fax 250-383-6804 E-mail sales@trafford.com
Web site www.trafford.com TRAFFORD PUBLISHING IS A DIVISION OF TRAFFORD HOLDINGS LTD.
Trafford Catalogue #02-0454 www.trafford.com/robots/02-0454.html

10 9 8 7 6 5 4

To my wife Judy
and our wonderful
family. They make
the work worthwhile.

ACKNOWLEGEMENTS

I owe a great debt of gratitude to my family and friends who have encouraged me to push ahead with this book, and I thank them for their interest and support.

Until you try to write a book, you do not comprehend in the slightest what it takes in the way of technical and professional assistance to make it happen. I certainly have that understanding now, and I wish to express my appreciation to all those people who helped me with my creation.

Special thanks to special people are in order beginning with Larry Bell the former C.E.O. of VanCity Savings Credit Union who saw something others had missed. Thank you to Tom Hancock and his peers and staff at VanCity who have been part of this for nearly a decade now. Thanks to Preston Manning, Elizabeth Nickson and Herb Grubel for their encouragement.

The book, the software and the website (*www.smithman.net*) (never miss a chance) happened because of first rank professionals doing their magic on my behalf. They are Bruce Batchelor president of Trafford Publishing and Jennifer Taylor my Special Agent. The covers of this book were created by an ace designer, Victor Crapnell. Spreadsheet translation was by my favourite engineer with the iron ring, Carol Maas. The Visual Basic programming and website design is the excellent work of the Dynamic Duo, Norman Sim and Ken De'Ath.

Many people supplied ideas, insight, encouragement and editing skills. They are Gordon and Mary Jane Shaw, Frank Edgell, Tom Bazin, John Schreiner, Bob Baillie, Dr. Dave Godfrey, Troy Lanigan, Eric and Jennifer Verscheure and Rob Smith, M.B.A. My thanks to them all.

This book would not likely have been written but for the patience, dedication, loyalty and long and extra hours put in by my long-time assistant and good friend, LuAnn Olson. It's LuAnn who really runs this place, and I'm grateful.

Lastly, I'd like to recognize all those dedicated, hard working Canadian families doing their part to keep Canada a great place to live. It is a privilege to be able to pass on to those families with house mortgages the means to improve their wealth utilizing *The Smith Manoeuvre.*

Fraser Smith
Saanichton, B.C. September 2002

FOREWORD

In 1984, the Board of Directors of Vancouver City Savings determined to take steps to secure their dominant position in the British Columbia and Canadian credit union movement.

As Chief Executive Officer at the time, I felt it was propitious that Fraser Smith had targeted VanCity to champion his unique financial strategy for mortgage owners in Canada. The Smith Manoeuvre, as it was to become known, was simple and elegant. We attracted many new customers over the years by virtue of our support of the program.

My question back then still stands today – "Why isn't every Canadian making his mortgage tax deductible?" Perhaps the publishing of "The Smith Manoeuvre" will make it happen.

Larry Bell
Vancouver, B.C.

DISCLAIMER

The information contained in this book has been developed over several years of experience and is believed to be accurate and reliable. The reader is reminded that there may be variations in the interpretation of various laws and regulations in different jurisdictions because of the nature of the subject matter being dealt with.

The author and publisher specifically disclaim any liability arising from loss, personal or otherwise, incurred directly or indirectly as a consequence of the use and application of any of the information contained in this book. In no event will the author, publisher, or any distributor of this book be liable to the purchaser for any amount greater than the purchase price of this book.

This publication is sold with the understanding that neither the author nor the publisher is engaged in rendering legal, financial planning, investment, accounting, tax, or other professional assistance or advice. If legal, investment, financial planning, accounting, tax, or other professional assistance or advice is required, you should seek the services of a competent professional with the required qualifications.

CONTENTS

INTRODUCTION

On the average, the financial life of the average Canadian is, well, average. But you can't trust averages. When you are sitting on a block of ice with a bare ass, and your hair is on fire, on the average, you feel good.

If you have read this far, and are starting to realize that The Smith Manoeuvre is not the title of Robert Ludlum's latest novel, do not despair. Sometimes, real-life is more interesting than fiction.

Today you are going to learn how to re-engineer the way you deal with your house mortgage. When you implement the strategy you are about to discover, it will cause the taxman to send you tax refund cheques, big ones, each year until you die at age 130. The tax refund cheques come every year, they are free, there is no tax on them and it is all perfectly legal.

These are not small tax refunds. Your mortgage payments for a year total a huge number. As much as 70% or 80% of that huge number is the interest you are paying the bank. 80% of a huge number is also a huge number. Let's say it's $10,000 for our Mr. Average, Paul

Martine. Paul likes tax deductions. Every year he buys a $10,000 RRSP. (He has to first earn an extra $20,000 for the year so he can give up half to all the governments who want all their taxes, leaving him $10,000 to buy his RRSP). So Paul buys his $10,000 RRSP and claims a $10,000 tax deduction when he submits his income tax return. A few weeks later, Paul gets a lovely cheque from the taxman for $4,000 being 40% of the tax deduction he claimed. That's a 40% return on his "investment" which is excellent performance.

What Paul doesn't know is that hidden in his annual mortgage payments is another $10,000 tax deduction, which is free for the arranging. And he doesn't have to go and earn another $20,000 to get it. If he reads this book, he will learn how easy and inexpensive it is to convert an expense he is already paying, his mortgage interest, into a tax deduction that will yield equivalent benefits to what he would receive if he bought an RRSP. Not only that, once the conversion has been effected, the tax deductions will be automatic and free every year for as many years into the future as he still has a mortgage.

If you have a mortgage you could have all the same advantages as Paul Martine. But that's not all. Simultaneously you will begin now to build an investment portfolio of your own choosing. You will decide whether you want to invest in stocks, bonds, mutual funds, investment real estate, your own business or somebody else's business. These investments will be free and clear.

It sounds too good to be true. But before you adopt that assumption, consider that The Smith Manoeuvre has been operating continuously since 1984, tax lawyers from several of Canada's top law firms have confirmed to several large financial institutions that this is a creative but legal financial strategy. Revenue Canada auditors have interviewed me and my Manoeuvre in my office and hundreds of people are enjoying the luxury of The Smith Manoeuvre with more being added every month.

You may well ask, "Why isn't every Canadian doing this?" The answer is that I haven't met them all yet. The next best thing was to write this book, explain how it works and how to arrange these free benefits for your family. It's my gift to Canadians. I take great pleasure in the knowledge that many who read this book will be empowered to substantially improve the financial life of their family utilizing these tools of the wealthy. A little knowledge is a magnificent thing in the hands of the motivated. So do order the software (see the last page of this book) so you can run various versions of your own numbers and circumstances. Then, go to a financial planner and ask him or her to confirm the validity of the assumptions and projections. Then retain him or her to implement The Smith Manoeuvre for you. You will be glad you did.

Fraser Smith
Saanichton, B.C.

1

IN A NUTSHELL

What is The Smith Manoeuvre?

The Smith Manoeuvre is a creative, legal financial strategy that will generate free annual tax refunds for many years into the future for any Canadian who has a house mortgage. Your mortgage will melt away as fast as your investment portfolio grows. The wealthy class has used this strategy for years, with the blessing of the taxman. This book extends the knowledge and provides instructions to all the rest of us. It will make a huge positive impact on your family's net worth.

The Smith Manoeuvre converts non-deductible interest debt (bad debt) to tax deductible interest debt (good debt). Bad-debt loans such as car loans, vacation loans and especially home mortgage loans, cost Canadians huge amounts of non-deductible interest every year. If this same amount of interest was a tax deduction, impressive tax refund cheques would start appearing as free gifts from the taxman each year.

If you have interest to pay anyway, why not at least convert it to interest that gives you generous, free, gratis, no charge, tax paid gifts each year? This gift will be courtesy of the Canada Customs and Revenue Agency (CCRA) (formerly known as Revenue Canada). They will be quite happy to send you a big, juicy refund cheque every year until you die at age 130. You only need to take the time to reorganize the structure of the debt you are already carrying. Then the tax refund cheques start coming. Free. No charge. Gifts.

Just How Large Will These Cheques from the Taxman Be?

The interest on a new $100,000 mortgage at 7% would be $6,852 in interest expense in the first year, non-deductible. If this mortgage was a tax-deductible mortgage, and if you were at the 40% tax bracket, you would receive a cheque from the taxman for $6,852 x .40 = $2,740 as a gift.

If your mortgage were $200,000 at 7%, your free gift from CCRA would be double at $5,481. Free. No tax to pay on the gift either. It is truly free, no strings attached. Deductible interest is far better than non-deductible interest.

There is Another Large Advantage

If you are a Canadian using The Smith Manoeuvre, in addition to the gift of generous tax refunds, you will meet another objective common to all of us. You will become the owner of a portfolio of assets such as stocks, bonds, mutual funds and investment real estate. You could invest in your own business, or someone else's business. You will choose the investments. The assets will be free and clear – they will be unencumbered. There will be no margin calls. The purchase of these new assets will begin *now*, the generation of tax deductions will begin *now*, and the non-deductible debt will begin to disappear *now*.

Why Isn't Every Canadian Doing This?

The only ones who aren't are the ones who have not yet read this book. If you have friends, relatives, co-workers or children who have a mortgage or any bad debt, you might suggest they order this book, or why not give them a copy as a gift?

Are There Any Rules?

In Canada, when you borrow to buy a car, to go on a vacation, to consolidate your consumer loans or to buy your home, you are prevented by law from claiming the annual interest expense of these loans as a tax deduction. Americans generally can deduct this interest at tax time, and accordingly they pay less tax than we Canadians. This is a major factor when trying to figure out why an American lives to such a higher standard than his Canadian counterpart.

Sounds like we are doomed. But just a minute. Some types of interest in Canada *are* tax deductible. If the money you borrow is for the purpose of investing, where you expect to earn income, then the interest on *that* loan *is* deductible.

Remember this - the test for deductibility of interest is: *What did you do with the money when you borrowed it?* Bought a car? Forget it. Bought a home? No dice. The loan interest in these examples is *not* deductible because the purpose of the borrowing was *not* to invest, it was for consumption.

So we have a problem. You already own a house with a mortgage, which is not deductible. Most of my clients come to me carrying perhaps the largest debt they will own in their lifetime, their mortgage and it's non-deductible.

You already have the mortgage - is it too late for you?

Not if you know how to utilize The Smith Manoeuvre.

What Should You Do?

You already have the mortgage loan, or the car loan, or maybe a consumer loan or line of credit, maybe credit card debt - all non-deductible interest loans. You would also be glad to be building an investment portfolio if you could, but you feel you need to get your debt paid off first.

Your plan is to get the debt down over the next few years, then you expect to be able to start an investment program. This is a significant recommendation for Canadians made by Garth Turner, one of Canada's pre-eminent financial gurus. His excellent book *The Strategy* is a must read for Canadians serious about their financial well-being. Garth's website address is *www.garth.ca.*

Most of the financial planning books tell you to do it that way. Pay off your mortgage, then start an investment program. Your friends, family, neighbours and work mates are all doing it that way, so it must be right.

There is a much better way. Organize your financial life to set up The Smith Manoeuvre.

Step 1 Read this book

Step 2 Order THE SMITHMAN CALCULATOR so that you can do calculations based on your own financial circumstances (see the last page of this book for ordering instructions, or go to *www.smithman.net*).

Step 3 Ask your financial planner to organize The Smith Manoeuvre for you.

Step 4 If you don't have a financial planner, think seriously about getting one. Find one who implements The Smith Manoeuvre for his or her clients. See the Appendix for suggestions on locating a financial planner. Updated on website.

Step 5 If you are a risk taker, just ask your banker to set up The Smith Manoeuvre banking procedure for you. I personally believe it's better to have a third party agent, a financial planner, organizing the details for you. You don't remove your own tonsils. Non-deductible debt can be just as injurious to your health. Get thee to a planner.

Step 6 If you want to do it yourself, spend extra time with Chapter 5, "Implementation".

Summary

Most Canadians would like:

1. To get rid of their house mortgage as soon as possible.
2. To own lots of investments to ensure their financial future.

Most Canadians attack these two wishes sequentially, and most financial planners encourage them to do so – pay off their mortgage, then start an investment program.

What's wrong with that?

It is better than doing nothing, but to take 15 or 20 years of your life to deal with the mortgage before you begin to invest loses you 15 or 20 years of compounding time in your investment portfolio.

The Smith Manoeuvre has you getting rid of your old mortgage very quickly while *simultaneously* starting your lifelong investment program – *now*. We can accomplish these two objectives at the same time, starting *now*. Wealth creation takes time. The Smith Manoeuvre gives you the gift of all the time you have left in your life, to build your wealth while getting rid of that bad-debt mortgage.

In addition, free, new money from the taxman begins to be generated *now*. *Now* is very important. It matters not how old you are, how wealthy you are or whether you're a socialist or a free-enterpriser. The bad news is that you have the wrong kind of debt, and it's killing you slowly. The good news is that it is easy to fix.

Take action *now*. Remember that old saying, "Today is the first day of the rest of your financial life." You can optimize your financial future by engaging the power of The Smith Manoeuvre. Do it *now*.

2

IN THE BEGINNING

It all began in Vancouver

In 1980, long before it was fashionable, my wife Judy and I went in for financial planning. Like the Remington shaver guy, Victor Kiam, "I liked it so much I joined the company" and I apprenticed the personal financial planning business. In 1981, with four great friends and partners, Granville West was founded in Vancouver, and we never looked back. Granville West has become a powerful Vancouver corporate entity specializing in financial planning, insurance and benefits plans. In 1992, Judy and I moved to Saanichton, BC on Vancouver Island where I developed Smith Consulting Group and KittyHawk Securities.

I was fascinated by the fact that Americans were able to deduct the interest on their loans, including their house mortgage loans. One reason that our friends in the USA enjoy a higher life style than we do, is because the American home owner has a huge tax deduction to claim each and every year that he owns a mortgage. (An American does start to lose some deductions on anything over a million-dollar mortgage.)

In Canada, house mortgages do not give rise to deductible interest for all but a small percentage of the population. In an attempt to find out more about the rules of tax deductibility, I spent some time with the Tax Act, which is a brutal read.

Who Enjoys Tax Deductible Mortgages in Canada?

The truly wealthy.

Plus my clients, most of whom are just ordinary taxpayers like most Canadians.

Wealthy people, and all of my clients, are just as likely as you are to have a mortgage on their home. The difference is that the monthly interest portion of their mortgage is tax deductible, and yours is not.

We can learn much from the wealthy. First, they understand leverage. They use OPM – Other People's Money to increase their own wealth. Secondly, any debt they do take on generates big tax deductions because they only borrow to invest.

You will recall that the test for deductibility is "what did you do with the money when you borrowed it." Borrow to invest and you can deduct the interest.

It is fashionable in some quarters to denigrate the use of leverage to increase one's wealth, but if you have a house mortgage, you are leveraging. You may have put down as little as 5% to buy a house, borrowing 95% from "Other People" to complete the purchase. And good for you. If you borrow to invest, you are leveraging.

There is a pattern emerging here. Wealthy people intentionally pay for houses, cars, and vacations with their after-tax cash. The not so wealthy, which is most of us, borrow the money to buy our houses, cars and vacations. We do it backwards. At great expense to our future net worth, and our future financial well-being.

Wealthy people borrow money too, but they use it to buy investments such as rental real estate, mutual funds, stocks and bonds. They will also borrow to buy a piece of somebody else's business, or to put into their own business. The rest of the population, which is most of the people in Canada, don't have much money left over at the end of the month with which to invest. When you are paying as much as half of your income in taxes of many kinds, and when you are paying those huge amounts of interest to the bank for your mortgage every month, most Canadians find it very difficult to consider the purchase of investments. So they wait for a better time, such as when the mortgage is retired.

This really hurts your chances of improving your future net worth at a decent rate because the time value of owning investments dictates that the sooner you own them, the more they will compound their value as the years go by. We need a program that allows us get rid of our non-deductible house mortgage as fast as possible and simultaneously we need to be building an investment portfolio. Americans tend to do both things at the same time. Canadians usually wait until the mortgage is gone before they start investing. As you will see, if you use The Smith Manoeuvre, you will be able to do even better than our friends south of the border. You might even move into the wealthy category if you do it right. The Smith Manoeuvre will make this all possible for you.

The wealthy Canadian example, let's call him Eric, may start with a non-deductible loan to buy his house, just like you. But very quickly, his highly paid accountants and lawyers show him one of the tricks of the trade – how to convert the bad-interest loan to a good-interest loan.

Example: Eric may have a new house with a new and non-deductible mortgage for $200,000, just like you. Assume he also has $200,000 worth of mutual funds he has gathered over the years. Eric's tax accountant will be quick to suggest that his client sell his mutual funds, and with the $200,000 cheque he receives, Eric will pay off his brand new mortgage today.

Tomorrow, he will go back to the banker, borrow back $200,000 using the house as collateral, and he will use the borrowed money to buy back $200,000 worth of mutual funds. Eric still has his house, his $200,000 mutual funds and a $200,000 loan, but one important thing is different. Because he borrowed to invest, he has just converted $200,000 of debt from bad debt (non-deductible interest), to good debt (deductible interest). Eric may have some taxes to pay on the sale of the mutual funds, and he may have some commissions to pay his planner for the sale and re-purchase of his mutual funds, but these costs are small potatoes compared to the huge tax deductions he will be getting every year for years into the future.

At 7%, Eric will have a $14,000 tax deduction this year, next year, and every year that he has the loan, probably to 130 years of age. You won't. Unless you decide to learn how to do The Smith Manoeuvre.

Wealthy people tend not to pay off deductible loans. Why would they? At the 50% tax bracket, the tax department will be sending our wealthy example a cheque for $7,000, tax-free. Every year. You won't get a cheque, even though you both paid the same amount of interest on your loans. The cheque from the tax department is free. It is a gift. There is no tax on it. You can do anything you want with it. It is legal. In fact it is encouraged.

You are paying the interest as part of your monthly mortgage payment every month anyway. Why not make it tax deductible? Embrace The Smith Manoeuvre, and it will become deductible.

The Rich Get Richer

It doesn't seem too fair, but rather than whimper, let's learn from the wealthy and do our best to emulate their methods. In our example, the debt conversion was done in one day, but there is nothing to prevent persons of more modest means from accomplishing the same results over a longer period of time, by the month. If you own paid up mutual funds, you should consider selling them, reduce your mortgage, then borrow back the same amount to purchase new mutual funds. Because you borrowed to invest, the interest will be deductible.

You may have some tax to pay if your mutual funds have grown in value and you may have commissions to pay for the sale and re-purchase of the funds. This negative issue will be modest in comparison to the advantages that accrue through tax savings over time.

There are traps to fall into and rules of order to follow so do yourself a favour and retain the services of a financial planner to ensure you optimize your opportunity. For instance, there are rules against selling securities one day then re-purchasing the same securities within 30 days. If you set your borrowing facilities up in the wrong manner, you could foul up your claim for deductibility as far as the tax department is concerned. It can hurt you to try and do this by yourself. Attempting your own financial planning in these modern times is as dangerous to your health as is taking out your own appendix. Find a real financial planner, one with a designation after his name. These are registered and certified planners who take courses and pass exams. Appendix 'A' includes a list of Canadian organizations that supervise and regulate a membership of individuals who have attained the proficiency levels required to utilize the designations of that institution. When you find one you like, get a resume and check with some of the planner's current clients to whom the planner will be pleased to refer you.

This would be a bad juncture in your life to try to do it yourself.

The Objective of The Smith Manoeuvre

The wealthy use leverage, and so do you. Leverage is simply borrowing to invest. The debt of the wealthy generates deductible interest to reduce their tax, which increases their cash flow. They get richer. Your debt, your mortgage, is paid for with your after-tax dollars, and generates no deductible interest. The task at hand is to learn how to do what the wealthy do – convert the mortgage loan from bad debt with non-deductible interest, to good debt where the interest is tax deductible. The Smith Manoeuvre is a debt conversion strategy.

We can turn your mortgage into the good kind.

3

HOW DOES THE SMITH MANOEUVRE WORK?

The Smith Manoeuvre works by converting the bad debt you already have such as your home mortgage, into a good-debt investment loan. Any bad-debt loan can and should be converted into a good-debt loan, but for the purposes of this book we will almost always use an example of an average family, with an average house, an average mortgage and an average income. Conversion of other kinds of non-deductible debt will be covered at the end of this chapter.

Everyone has a different set of financial circumstances to deal with. This book can teach using examples, but it can't produce results specific to the financial circumstances of your own family.

To solve the problem you will be able to utilize my proprietary software THE SMITHMAN CALCULATOR referenced in the first chapter. A full range of input variables makes it possible to produce calculations specific to your own personal financial situation at this time of your life. You can play what-if for hours to help you compare various mortgage/investment strategies. There is an order form on the last page of this book for you to photocopy, or you can print off an order form at *www.smithman.net*.

Let's do a Couple of Examples:

We will input imaginary numbers for two Canadian families using THE SMITHMAN CALCULATOR.

The first case is the Black family, followed by the Browns. The objective in each case is to have the computer compare the financial difference between utilizing The Smith Manoeuvre and doing things the same old way. You will be surprised by the results.

The Blacks are an under 40 family with both parents working with a total of $100,000 per year joint income. They have a new house and a new mortgage for $200,000. They have two kids so they don't have many other assets yet, but they do manage to put away $500 per month into CSB's, term deposits and GIC's, being conservative folk.

Their program has allowed them to put away a total of $30,000 over the years in CSB's and term deposits as an emergency fund, and they have a $20,000 GIC maturing in 6 months, which is their nest egg. They have some other assets and some RRSPs but these assets are not considered for this exercise. David Chilton wrote a wonderful best seller entitled *The Wealthy Barber* in which the virtues of investing 10% of one's gross income are demonstrated. At $500/mth or $6,000 per year (6% of gross income) going into CSB's, term deposits and GIC's the Blacks are fairly short of David Chilton's target for them of 10% per year, but kids really are expensive, and taxes of all kinds take nearly 50% of everything this family earns.

Most financial planners would be complimentary of this family's efforts thus far.

Summary:

$200,000	mortgage loan amount
40%	marginal tax rate
25 yrs	amortization period
5 yrs	term
7.0%	interest rate of the mortgage
5.0%	interest rate of borrowing to invest

$100,000	total family gross income
10.0%	assumed annual average rate of return on investments
$ 500	monthly purchase of CSB's, term deposits and GIC's
$ 30,000	current value of accumulated CSB's and term deposits
$ 20,000	GIC nest egg, maturing in 6 months.

The Plain Jane Smith Manoeuvre

The Plain Jane Smith Manoeuvre describes the financial strategy of setting up a Smith Manoeuvre at a bank or credit union to do a simple conversion of your debt from bad debt to good debt, in two steps:

Step I

Borrowing back and investing the monthly principal reduction that occurs as you make your monthly mortgage payments over the months remaining on your mortgage. Borrowing the money back creates an investment loan and the interest on this investment loan is tax deductible.

You are building an investment portfolio with the borrowed money.

Step II

Each year, when your tax refund arrives, you use this free money to make an extra payment against your mortgage, then you immediately re-borrow and invest the same amount.

That's it. That's all it takes to start the Plain Jane Smith Manoeuvre working for you.

What Difference Does it Make?

Examining the results of Step I using THE SMITHMAN CALCULATOR reveals the following:

Results of Step I *Re-borrow the monthly principal reduction of your mortgage and invest the loan proceeds. (Figure 3.1)*

a. When we run THE SMITHMAN CALCULATOR and check-mark the first box for Step I we notice that because of The Smith

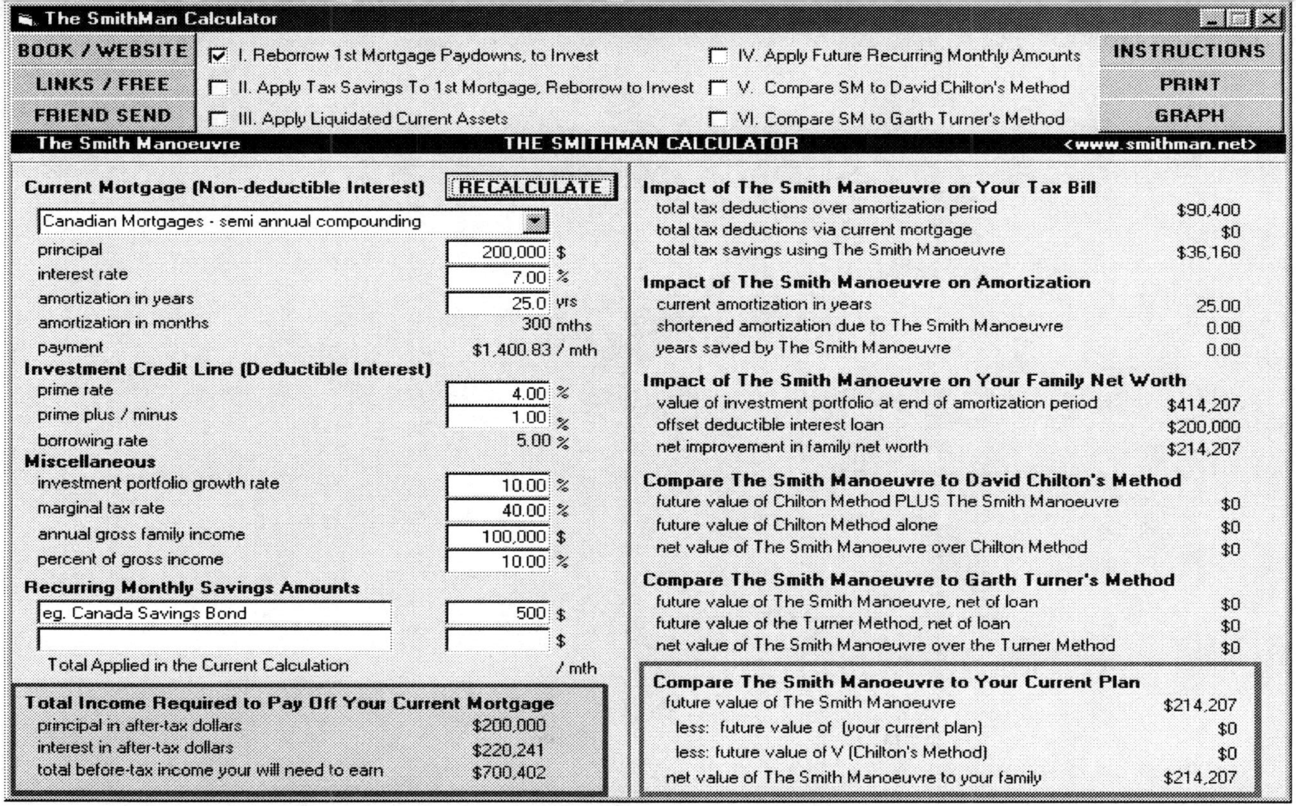

The SmithMan Calculator

BOOK / WEBSITE | LINKS / FREE | FRIEND SEND

- [x] I. Reborrow 1st Mortgage Paydowns, to Invest
- [ ] II. Apply Tax Savings To 1st Mortgage, Reborrow to Invest
- [ ] III. Apply Liquidated Current Assets
- [ ] IV. Apply Future Recurring Monthly Amounts
- [ ] V. Compare SM to David Chilton's Method
- [ ] VI. Compare SM to Garth Turner's Method

INSTRUCTIONS | PRINT | GRAPH

The Smith Manoeuvre — **THE SMITHMAN CALCULATOR** — **<www.smithman.net>**

Current Mortgage (Non-deductible Interest) RECALCULATE

Canadian Mortgages - semi annual compounding

principal	200,000	$
interest rate	7.00	%
amortization in years	25.0	yrs
amortization in months	300	mths
payment	$1,400.83	/ mth
Investment Credit Line (Deductible Interest)		
prime rate	4.00	%
prime plus / minus	1.00	%
borrowing rate	5.00	%
Miscellaneous		
investment portfolio growth rate	10.00	%
marginal tax rate	40.00	%
annual gross family income	100,000	$
percent of gross income	10.00	%
Recurring Monthly Savings Amounts		
eg. Canada Savings Bond	500	$
		$
Total Applied in the Current Calculation		/ mth

Total Income Required to Pay Off Your Current Mortgage	
principal in after-tax dollars	$200,000
interest in after-tax dollars	$220,241
total before-tax income your will need to earn	$700,402

Impact of The Smith Manoeuvre on Your Tax Bill	
total tax deductions over amortization period	$90,400
total tax deductions via current mortgage	$0
total tax savings using The Smith Manoeuvre	$36,160
Impact of The Smith Manoeuvre on Amortization	
current amortization in years	25.00
shortened amortization due to The Smith Manoeuvre	0.00
years saved by The Smith Manoeuvre	0.00
Impact of The Smith Manoeuvre on Your Family Net Worth	
value of investment portfolio at end of amortization period	$414,207
offset deductible interest loan	$200,000
net improvement in family net worth	$214,207
Compare The Smith Manoeuvre to David Chilton's Method	
future value of Chilton Method PLUS The Smith Manoeuvre	$0
future value of Chilton Method alone	$0
net value of The Smith Manoeuvre over Chilton Method	$0
Compare The Smith Manoeuvre to Garth Turner's Method	
future value of The Smith Manoeuvre, net of loan	$0
future value of the Turner Method, net of loan	$0
net value of The Smith Manoeuvre over the Turner Method	$0

Compare The Smith Manoeuvre to Your Current Plan	
future value of The Smith Manoeuvre	$214,207
less: future value of (your current plan)	$0
less: future value of V (Chilton's Method)	$0
net value of The Smith Manoeuvre to your family	$214,207

Figure 3.1

Manoeuvre, nearly half of the above interest expense of $220,241 will turn into tax-deductible interest for the Blacks, a total of $90,400. At the 40% tax bracket, this family will have tax refund cheques totalling $36,160. Free. Not bad for simply rearranging their financing using The Smith Manoeuvre.

b. In addition, assuming for instance that the re-borrowed money was invested in mutual funds earning 10% per year, the pool of funds would stand at $414,207. *These investments are free and clear.* These investments are also liquid depending on what you decide to buy for your investment portfolio.

To be fair, the original example showed zero debt after 300 months (and zero investments) so we should offset the $200,000 investment loan we are still carrying 25 years later to yield a net improvement of $414,207 - $200,000 = $214,207.

Note on Step I

This mortgage will require the owner to pay back $200,000 principal plus 220,241 dollars in interest (non-deductible) for a total of 420,241 dollars. But house mortgages are paid with after-tax dollars, so to understand the true pain of owning a mortgage we need to look at the before-tax cost of the mortgage. This family, at the 40% tax bracket, will have to earn $700,402 to pay off their modest $200,000 mortgage. Nearly three quarters of a million dollars. Do you see why your mortgage is killing you?

Results of Step II *Apply tax refunds against the first mortgage, then re-borrow and invest. (Figure 3.2)*

a. The tax savings resulting from the deductible interest expense being claimed on your income tax return are found money. As found money, generated by The Smith Manoeuvre, we have no difficulty getting agreement from our clients that these tax savings should be applied against the first mortgage, and the reduction is immediately re-borrowed and invested. Make this agreement with yourself – now.

b. After Step II is check-marked on the model contained in THE SMITHMAN

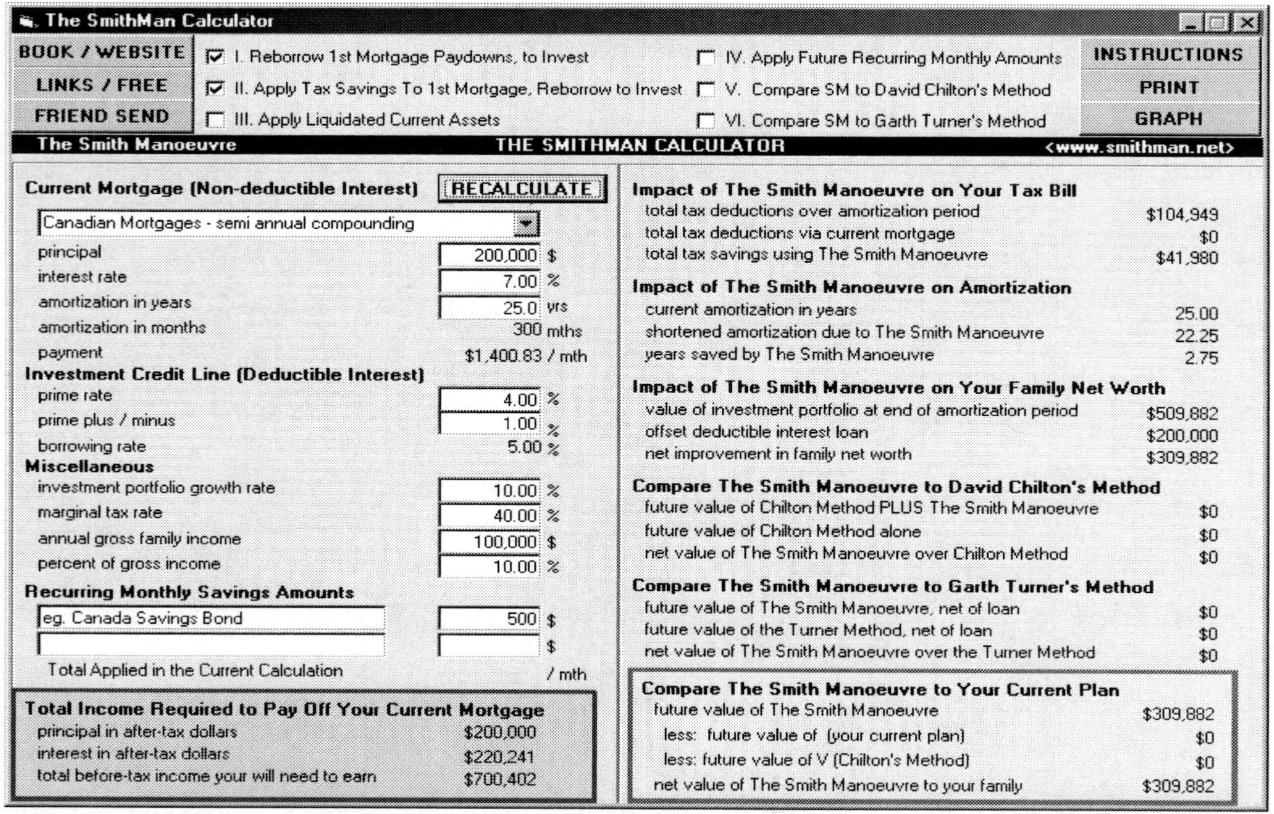

The SmithMan Calculator

BOOK / WEBSITE | LINKS / FREE | FRIEND SEND

- [x] I. Reborrow 1st Mortgage Paydowns, to Invest
- [x] II. Apply Tax Savings To 1st Mortgage, Reborrow to Invest
- [ ] III. Apply Liquidated Current Assets
- [ ] IV. Apply Future Recurring Monthly Amounts
- [ ] V. Compare SM to David Chilton's Method
- [ ] VI. Compare SM to Garth Turner's Method

INSTRUCTIONS | PRINT | GRAPH

The Smith Manoeuvre — THE SMITHMAN CALCULATOR — <www.smithman.net>

Current Mortgage (Non-deductible Interest) RECALCULATE

Canadian Mortgages - semi annual compounding

principal	200,000	$
interest rate	7.00	%
amortization in years	25.0	yrs
amortization in months	300	mths
payment	$1,400.83	/ mth
Investment Credit Line (Deductible Interest)		
prime rate	4.00	%
prime plus / minus	1.00	%
borrowing rate	5.00	%
Miscellaneous		
investment portfolio growth rate	10.00	%
marginal tax rate	40.00	%
annual gross family income	100,000	$
percent of gross income	10.00	%
Recurring Monthly Savings Amounts		
eg. Canada Savings Bond	500	$
		$
Total Applied in the Current Calculation		/ mth

Total Income Required to Pay Off Your Current Mortgage

principal in after-tax dollars	$200,000
interest in after-tax dollars	$220,241
total before-tax income your will need to earn	$700,402

Impact of The Smith Manoeuvre on Your Tax Bill

total tax deductions over amortization period	$104,949
total tax deductions via current mortgage	$0
total tax savings using The Smith Manoeuvre	$41,980

Impact of The Smith Manoeuvre on Amortization

current amortization in years	25.00
shortened amortization due to The Smith Manoeuvre	22.25
years saved by The Smith Manoeuvre	2.75

Impact of The Smith Manoeuvre on Your Family Net Worth

value of investment portfolio at end of amortization period	$509,882
offset deductible interest loan	$200,000
net improvement in family net worth	$309,882

Compare The Smith Manoeuvre to David Chilton's Method

future value of Chilton Method PLUS The Smith Manoeuvre	$0
future value of Chilton Method alone	$0
net value of The Smith Manoeuvre over Chilton Method	$0

Compare The Smith Manoeuvre to Garth Turner's Method

future value of The Smith Manoeuvre, net of loan	$0
future value of the Turner Method, net of loan	$0
net value of The Smith Manoeuvre over the Turner Method	$0

Compare The Smith Manoeuvre to Your Current Plan

future value of The Smith Manoeuvre	$309,882
less: future value of (your current plan)	$0
less: future value of V (Chilton's Method)	$0
net value of The Smith Manoeuvre to your family	$309,882

Figure 3.2

CALCULATOR, we see that the tax deductions increase to $104,949, thus the tax savings refund cheque rises as well, to $41,980, being 40% of the deduction.

c. The mutual fund account grows even more, and compounds rapidly, to $509,882.

   We still should offset the fact that we have a $200,000 tax-deductible loan at the bank, which leaves a net improvement in net worth of $309,882. Free. No charge.

d. As a bonus, the new money available from tax refunds, when used to reduce the first mortgage, reduces the 25-year amortization period to 22.25 years.

e. THE SMITHMAN CALCULATOR allows you to graph the results of your various inputs. Figure 3.3 is the related graph to Figure 3.2. Notice that the tax deductions paid against the mortgage have reduced the amortization period by 2.75 years.

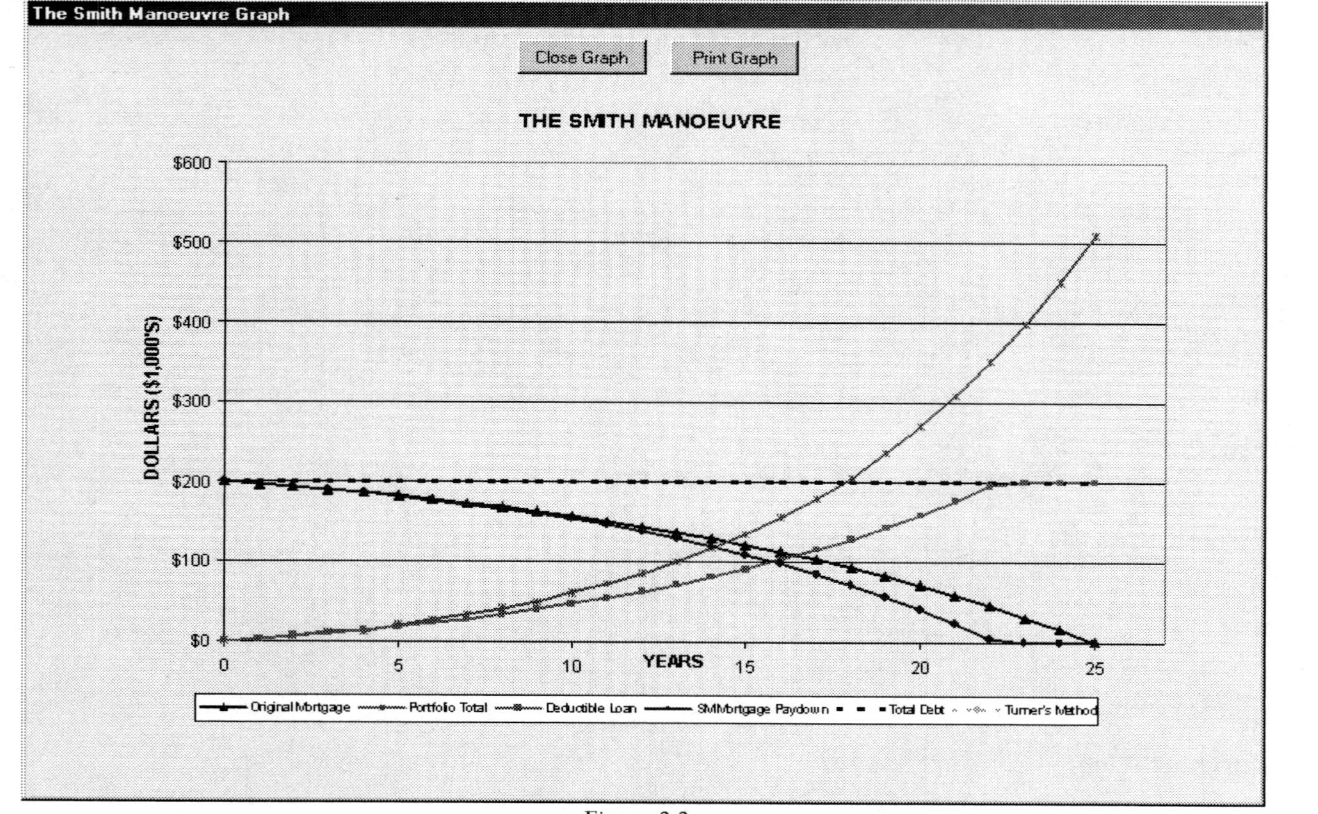
The Smith Manoeuvre Graph
Close Graph
Print Graph
THE SMITH MANOEUVRE
DOLLARS ($1,000'S)
$600
$500
$400
$300
$200
$100
$0
0
5
10
YEARS
15
20
25
Original Mortgage
Portfolio Total
Deductible Loan
SMMortgage Paydown
Total Debt
Turner's Method

Figure 3.3

Note on Step II

These improvements in your family's net worth needed no money from your income. The improvements to the net worth of the Black family, more than $300,000 net, are free to them. This could be your family. Another part of this free increase in wealth is because of free tax deductions that are used to pay down the mortgage, which is then re-borrowed and invested. Part of the increase results from the well understood concept that if you will invest for the long term, your investment gains will be higher than your borrowing costs, especially if your borrowing is for tax deductible purposes.

The salient difference between The Smith Manoeuvre and most other personal investment strategies is that The Smith Manoeuvre brings new money, free, to your family to allow you to speed up the reduction of your non-deductible loans, followed by immediate re-borrowing of the amount paid down. The interest expense of this re-borrowing is tax deductible.

That Old Bugbear, Debt

So I have not helped you with your debt. But a different indicator, net worth, is how government, business and wealthy people keep score, not the debt or lack of it. Debt is but one factor in the measurement of wealth. Proper and judicious utilization of debt is the hallmark of successful governments, vibrant businesses and wealthy individuals. You have debt too, just like the aforementioned groups. The difference is, theirs is tax deductible and yours is not. The effect is hugely negative for you, hugely positive for them.

Too much debt, deductible or not is a big mistake. Look at what successive governments under Trudeau, Mulroney and Chretien have done to our country. Governments in Canada have run up huge mountains of debt in your name and mine – about three quarters of a trillion dollars of it. That's **750 thousand million dollars**. Or 750 billion dollars. It's $750,000,000,000. It's a fantastic amount of money. That's *your* debt, and the debt of your kids, borrowed by successive governments, Liberal and Conservative. Before Trudeau, our governments were essentially operating with modest debt because at least they alternated deficit years with surplus years. The national deficit is the difference between two numbers. The first is the amount of money the government spends each year including those dollars wasted, paid out in grants, subsidies and loans, plus any payola required to grease the corruption game of which we seem to have a lot under the current government. The second number is the amount of money the government extorts from you in all the various kinds of taxes it arbitrarily imposes on you. The shortfall each year is added to the national debt. We have had so many bad years with large deficits that we now sit at about 750 billion dollars in debt. It's a crime.

In the main, the prime ministers prior to Trudeau ran the government house like you run your house – within their means. Trudeau ended that. Now we have a heavily mortgaged Canada, and our kids and you and I will have to pay it back. To be fair, Paul Martin has tried to stop the deficit train, but most of his surpluses have been engineered by increasing your tax bill.

Have you Heard of Tax Freedom Day?

Mr. Martin makes loud noises about reductions in income tax and some other taxes, but makes no noise about the taxes he increased. He gets his surplus by taxing you more. The evidence is in the annual calculation of Tax Freedom Day by the Fraser Institute (*www.fraserinstitute.ca*). Tax Freedom Day occurs on the day of the year that you cease to work for all the governments to pay all the taxes, so that you can start working for the benefit of you and your family. And taxes are sucking you dry. Last year, in 2001, Tax Freedom Day didn't arrive until June 26th – believe it or not. Four days short of half a year! 48.493% of a year! But guess what. Tax Freedom Day this year, 2002, was two days later than last year – 49.041% of a year. So taxes went up. Nice trick. The sly fox tricks the dumb peasants one more time. It's true that Tax Freedom Day includes all 3 levels of government, so Paul will say that the increase comes from the provinces and the municipalities. They will say it is because of reduced transfer payments from Paul, or by off loading budget from the federal government to the provinces, who in turn off load to the municipalities.

There are three levels of government, sometimes more, but there is only one taxpayer – you.

The feds are the main problem, so do your part to change the government. And we just keep voting them back in. Don't you wish the Alliance and the Conservatives would get it together?

Like the government, companies and wealthy folk are not immune to forgetting the rules when it comes to the use of debt – too much debt can bite.

The point is this – you already have the debt. My thesis is simply that you can pick up large improvements in net worth for your family by *converting* the debt you already have. *The Smith Manoeuvre does not require you to increase your debt.*

Even if your debt is reasonable in the amount of it, if it's standard home mortgage debt, it's the wrong kind of debt. The negative effect of debt is offset in magnificent fashion when you convert it from bad debt to good debt. Do this first. Get your debt converted using The Smith Manoeuvre, and once that's done, decide whether you want to hold it level for the next 100 years of your life, or reduce it. It won't take much time to convert, especially if you take the additional actions recommended further along in this book.

Let's look at what happens if this family makes a couple of additional moves to increase the outcome of their Smith Manoeuvre implementation.

The Enhanced Plain Jane Smith Manoeuvre

Steps I and II make up The Plain Jane Smith Manoeuvre. We can develop even larger net worth by adding two more steps that still don't require you to contribute any new money, nor does any new money need to be borrowed. All four steps together produce the Enhanced Plain Jane Smith Manoeuvre.

Step III

Reduce 1st mortgage using cash obtained by liquidating any available term deposits, CSB's, GIC's, or other paid up assets you own, *and then* borrow back the same amount to invest in replacement assets.

Step IV

Divert current monthly savings and investment plan amounts against the first mortgage, *and then* borrow back the same amount to invest.

Let's quantify the nice words with nice numbers using THE SMITHMAN CALCULATOR. By checking off the box at Step III, the numbers look rather dramatic. The excellent results stem from the benefits of liquidating the $30,000 and $20,000 assets and using the proceeds to reduce the first mortgage so the Blacks can re-borrow to invest.

Results of Step III *Lump sum reductions of first mortgage. (Figure 3.4)*

The tax deductions have now jumped from $104,949 to $195,552. At the 40% tax bracket, the tax savings have also jumped from $41,980 to $78,221 – nearly double.

In addition, instead of taking 25 years to get rid of the mortgage, it is now paid off in less than half the time at 12.08 years.

Best of all, the investment fund, purchased with borrowed funds so that the interest expense will be deductible, is much larger at $1,409,709. (You still need to offset $200,000 in recognition that we still have that deductible interest loan on

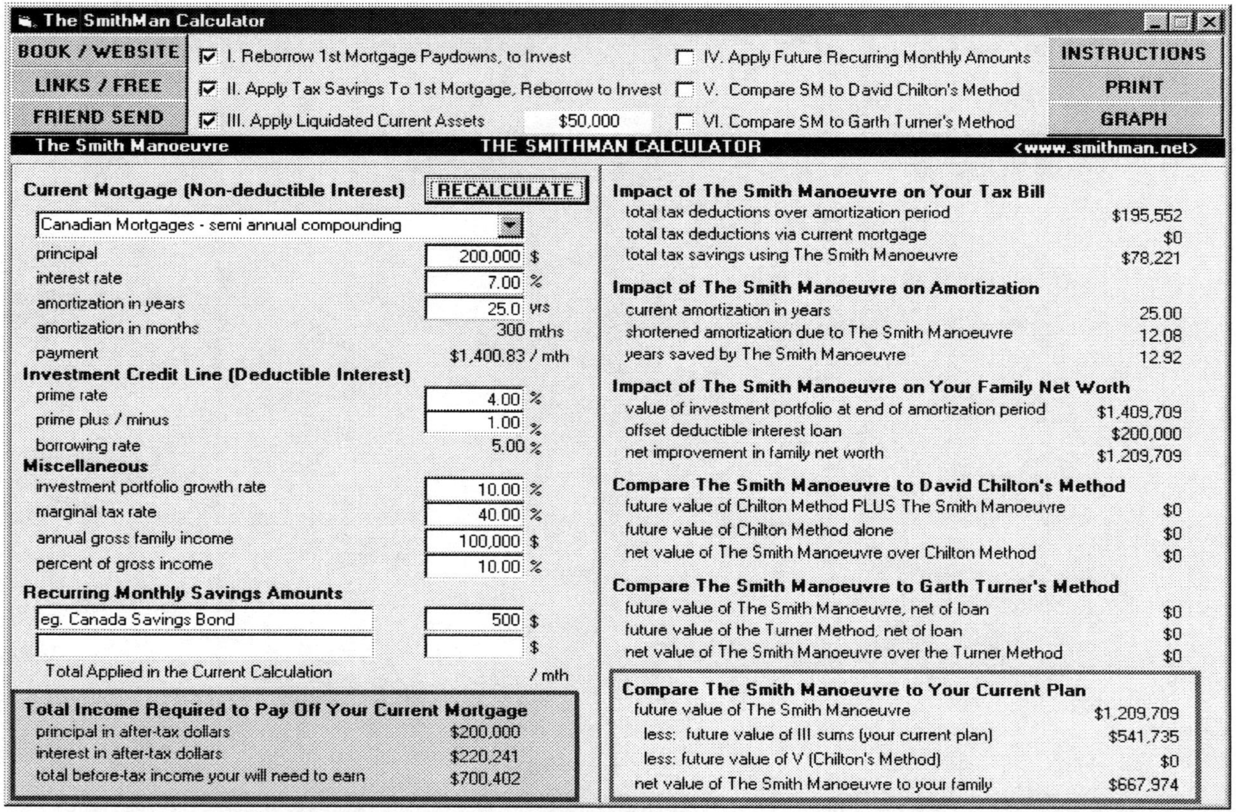

The SmithMan Calculator

BOOK / WEBSITE | LINKS / FREE | FRIEND SEND

- [x] I. Reborrow 1st Mortgage Paydowns, to Invest
- [x] II. Apply Tax Savings To 1st Mortgage, Reborrow to Invest
- [x] III. Apply Liquidated Current Assets $50,000
- [ ] IV. Apply Future Recurring Monthly Amounts
- [ ] V. Compare SM to David Chilton's Method
- [ ] VI. Compare SM to Garth Turner's Method

INSTRUCTIONS | PRINT | GRAPH

The Smith Manoeuvre — **THE SMITHMAN CALCULATOR** — **<www.smithman.net>**

Current Mortgage (Non-deductible Interest) RECALCULATE

Canadian Mortgages - semi annual compounding

principal	200,000	$
interest rate	7.00	%
amortization in years	25.0	yrs
amortization in months	300	mths
payment	$1,400.83	/ mth
Investment Credit Line (Deductible Interest)		
prime rate	4.00	%
prime plus / minus	1.00	%
borrowing rate	5.00	%
Miscellaneous		
investment portfolio growth rate	10.00	%
marginal tax rate	40.00	%
annual gross family income	100,000	$
percent of gross income	10.00	%
Recurring Monthly Savings Amounts		
eg. Canada Savings Bond	500	$
		$
Total Applied in the Current Calculation		/ mth

Total Income Required to Pay Off Your Current Mortgage	
principal in after-tax dollars	$200,000
interest in after-tax dollars	$220,241
total before-tax income your will need to earn	$700,402

Impact of The Smith Manoeuvre on Your Tax Bill	
total tax deductions over amortization period	$195,552
total tax deductions via current mortgage	$0
total tax savings using The Smith Manoeuvre	$78,221
Impact of The Smith Manoeuvre on Amortization	
current amortization in years	25.00
shortened amortization due to The Smith Manoeuvre	12.08
years saved by The Smith Manoeuvre	12.92
Impact of The Smith Manoeuvre on Your Family Net Worth	
value of investment portfolio at end of amortization period	$1,409,709
offset deductible interest loan	$200,000
net improvement in family net worth	$1,209,709
Compare The Smith Manoeuvre to David Chilton's Method	
future value of Chilton Method PLUS The Smith Manoeuvre	$0
future value of Chilton Method alone	$0
net value of The Smith Manoeuvre over Chilton Method	$0
Compare The Smith Manoeuvre to Garth Turner's Method	
future value of The Smith Manoeuvre, net of loan	$0
future value of the Turner Method, net of loan	$0
net value of The Smith Manoeuvre over the Turner Method	$0

Compare The Smith Manoeuvre to Your Current Plan	
future value of The Smith Manoeuvre	$1,209,709
less: future value of III sums (your current plan)	$541,735
less: future value of V (Chilton's Method)	$0
net value of The Smith Manoeuvre to your family	$667,974

Figure 2.4

the books.) With assets so high, you begin to realize what judicious use of leverage, or borrowing to invest, can do for your net worth.

To input lump sums at different months into the future, you will use a pop-up panel that appears when you click on Check Box III in THE SMITHMAN CALCULATOR software.

Note on Step III

After tax and after inflation, the CSB's and term deposits of $30,000 and the $20,000 GIC, are terrible investments. They earn a pittance in interest and attract full tax on the earnings, which has to be paid every year. Big tax on small interest is not good for your financial well being.

Many financial planners are still doling out the advice that you should have the equivalent of three to six months' income in a CSB or term deposit in case of an emergency. I've been at this business for over 20 years and I've met precious few families who have had such an emergency, number one. Number two, in case you do have an emergency, be covered by a "no-touchy" creditline to handle any such eventuality. It costs nothing unless you use it.

Number three, you should sell your CSB's and term deposits, apply the proceeds against your first mortgage, and borrow back the identical amount to purchase a real investment. If you invest in stocks, bonds, mutual funds, investment real estate, somebody else's business or your own business, the interest expense will be tax deductible. You are borrowing with the expectation of earning income from your investments.

You could do the conversion of the debt all in one day if you had enough assets. (The Blacks have $30,000 to deal with now, and $20,000 in six months.) By suppertime the Blacks will still be protected by their new creditline for that potential emergency, their mortgage will have been knocked down by $30,000, they will have bought back $30,000 in investments and because they borrowed to invest, the interest is tax deductible. Same for the $20,000 nest egg, six months from now.

So their debt stayed the same (bad debt down, good debt up by exactly the same amount), their mediocre assets in the form of CSB's, term deposits and GIC's have been replaced by some form of equities.

In addition the Blacks are generating free tax refund cheques because their mortgage interest, which they were paying anyway, has now been turned into tax deductible interest because the interest is being charged on an investment loan, not a housing loan.

Results of Step IV *Diverting monthly savings and investment amounts. (Figure 3.5)*

When we check-mark box IV on THE SMITHMAN CALCULATOR, we find all results in each category have increased again. Tax deductions have increased to $215,011 and the tax refunds will now be $86,005 instead of $78,221 after Step III.

We will be out of this mortgage in 8.08 years instead of 25 years.

Most amazingly, the mutual fund jumps to $2,162,770 (less the $200,000 loan we are still carrying because it is a tax deductible loan) for a total net worth improvement of $1,962,770 after 300 months. It may sound improbable, but you will find that the arithmetic is accurate.

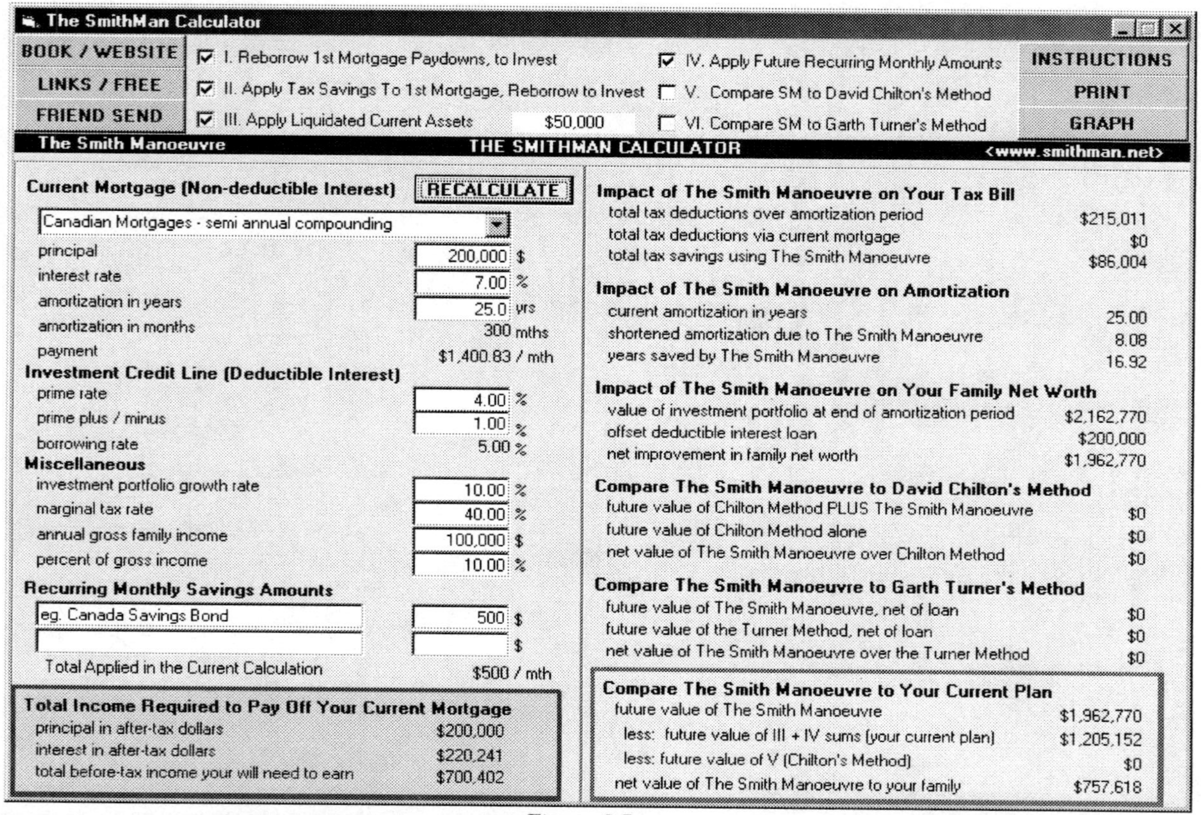

The SmithMan Calculator

BOOK / WEBSITE | LINKS / FREE | FRIEND SEND

- [x] I. Reborrow 1st Mortgage Paydowns, to Invest
- [x] II. Apply Tax Savings To 1st Mortgage, Reborrow to Invest
- [x] III. Apply Liquidated Current Assets $50,000
- [x] IV. Apply Future Recurring Monthly Amounts
- [ ] V. Compare SM to David Chilton's Method
- [ ] VI. Compare SM to Garth Turner's Method

INSTRUCTIONS | PRINT | GRAPH

The Smith Manoeuvre — THE SMITHMAN CALCULATOR — <www.smithman.net>

Current Mortgage (Non-deductible Interest) RECALCULATE

Canadian Mortgages - semi annual compounding

principal	200,000 $
interest rate	7.00 %
amortization in years	25.0 yrs
amortization in months	300 mths
payment	$1,400.83 / mth

Investment Credit Line (Deductible Interest)

prime rate	4.00 %
prime plus / minus	1.00 %
borrowing rate	5.00 %

Miscellaneous

investment portfolio growth rate	10.00 %
marginal tax rate	40.00 %
annual gross family income	100,000 $
percent of gross income	10.00 %

Recurring Monthly Savings Amounts

eg. Canada Savings Bond	500 $
	$
Total Applied in the Current Calculation	$500 / mth

Total Income Required to Pay Off Your Current Mortgage

principal in after-tax dollars	$200,000
interest in after-tax dollars	$220,241
total before-tax income your will need to earn	$700,402

Impact of The Smith Manoeuvre on Your Tax Bill

total tax deductions over amortization period	$215,011
total tax deductions via current mortgage	$0
total tax savings using The Smith Manoeuvre	$86,004

Impact of The Smith Manoeuvre on Amortization

current amortization in years	25.00
shortened amortization due to The Smith Manoeuvre	8.08
years saved by The Smith Manoeuvre	16.92

Impact of The Smith Manoeuvre on Your Family Net Worth

value of investment portfolio at end of amortization period	$2,162,770
offset deductible interest loan	$200,000
net improvement in family net worth	$1,962,770

Compare The Smith Manoeuvre to David Chilton's Method

future value of Chilton Method PLUS The Smith Manoeuvre	$0
future value of Chilton Method alone	$0
net value of The Smith Manoeuvre over Chilton Method	$0

Compare The Smith Manoeuvre to Garth Turner's Method

future value of The Smith Manoeuvre, net of loan	$0
future value of the Turner Method, net of loan	$0
net value of The Smith Manoeuvre over the Turner Method	$0

Compare The Smith Manoeuvre to Your Current Plan

future value of The Smith Manoeuvre	$1,962,770
less: future value of III + IV sums (your current plan)	$1,205,152
less: future value of V (Chilton's Method)	$0
net value of The Smith Manoeuvre to your family	$757,618

Figure 3.5

Note on Step IV

Over the years the Blacks have been saving 6% of their gross income to build up an emergency fund as recommended by a financial planner, plus a nest egg for the future. They are conservative, so the $500 per month is put into CSB's and term deposits in their emergency fund account and a portion of the cash is used to buy a GIC for their nest egg.

They should divert all these savings in order to reduce their first mortgage. As soon as this is done, they will borrow the same amount of money back from the bank, and get it invested. I will share my opinions on what kind of investments in the next chapter.

Comparing the Smith Manoeuvre to The Usual Way

The Blacks took four easy steps, reorganized their financial set up, converted their bad debt to the good kind, and now they are sitting on assets of nearly two million dollars.

Albert Einstein was asked what he would consider the eighth Wonder of the World, and apparently he said "compound interest". These numbers could be your numbers. It's easy to do. It's important to do.

We indicated that this was a comparison between two methods. Accordingly, we need to calculate where the Blacks would end up financially if they *did not* engage The Smith Manoeuvre. It's the difference that counts, because the results of both methods are exciting. One is more exciting than the other.

The following chart (Figure 3.6) summarizes and compares results for the difference in net worth for the Blacks doing it their way, and doing it The Smith Manoeuvre way.

What About Lower Income Families?

Here is a Smith Manoeuvre comparison for a younger family just getting in gear, the Browns.

$100,000	mortgage loan amount
30%	marginal tax rate
25 yrs	amortization period
5 yrs	term
7.0%	interest rate of the mortgage
5.0%	interest rate of borrowing to invest
$ 50,000	total family gross income

COMPARATIVE STRATEGY SUMMARIES FOR THE BLACK FAMILY

Fig 3.6

A. The usual way - pay off the mortgage to zero, while investing as much cash as possible for 25 years, at 10%.

	Debt		Tax			Net Worth After 25 Yrs.		
	Start	End	Deductions	Refunds	Time	Investments	Debt	Net Worth
Current mortgage	200,000	0	0	0	25 yrs	-	-	-
Current savings - $50,000	-	-	0	0	25 yrs	541,735	0	541,735
Monthly savings - $500	-	-	0	0	25 yrs	663,417	0	663,417
								$1,205,152

B. The Smith Manoeuvre way - convert the bad debt to good debt, re-borrow to invest, generate tax deductions to apply against the mortgage to increase deductible borrowing for investments, for 25 years at 10%.

	Debt Start	Debt End	Deductions	Refunds	Time	Investments	Debt	Net Worth
After Step I	200,000	200,000	90,400	36,120	25.00 yrs	414,207	200,000	214,207
After Step II	200,000	200,000	104,949	41,980	22.25 yrs	509,882	200,000	309,882
After Step III	200,000	200,000	195,552	78,221	12.08 yrs	1,409,709	200,000	1,209,709
After Step IV	200,000	200,000	215,011	86,005	8.08 yrs	2,162,770	200,000	1,962,770
								$1,962,770

C. Summary

Assuming the same starting position for each strategy regarding debt, time, investment rate of return, monthly investment amounts and current investment values, The Smith Manoeuvre has increased the future value of the Black's net worth from $1,205,152 to $1,962,770. This is a difference of $757,618, which represents an improvement of 62%.

10.0%	assumed annual average rate of return on investments
$ 200	monthly purchase of CSB's
$ 5,000	current value of accumulated CSB's.

The methodologies are exactly the same as the prior case. The results are even more striking for this lower income family on a proportionate basis, the Browns do better than the Blacks. The results of The Plain Jane Smith Manoeuvre (Step I and Step II) are free for the asking, courtesy of the taxman. The Enhanced Plain Jane Smith Manoeuvre (adding Steps III and IV) will improve the family's future net worth as well, simply by employing current assets and future planned savings in a more important way.

Note: In the Enhanced Plain Jane Smith Manoeuvre for both the Blacks and the Browns, the investment vehicles they owned that could be liquidated were Canada Savings Bonds, term deposits or Guaranteed Investment Certificates. Upon liquidation, so that proceeds could be utilized to pay down their existing first mortgage, the full value was available for mortgage reduction because these instruments have already paid income tax on their gains every year. It should be noted that if they were liquidating mutual funds, real estate or stock, there might be some income tax to pay in the year of sale, reducing by some amount, the funds available for mortgage reduction. This is another reason you should locate a financial planner to assist with the set-up of The Smith Manoeuvre (your banker likely won't have time to do these estimates for you).

The following chart (Figure 3.7) summarizes and compares results for the difference in net worth for the Browns doing it their way, and doing it The Smith Manoeuvre way.

This large improvement in this family's net worth is a consequence of free tax deductions generated by The Smith Manoeuvre, which are subsequently used to speed up the conversion period from bad debt to good debt, plus the resultant improvement in mortgage payment efficiency provided by the shortened amortization of the bad-debt mortgage.

Mortgage payment efficiency refers to the jump in the amount of principal reduction that occurs in the first and subsequent payments following a one-time payment of principal against a mortgage. The amount of the payments being

COMPARATIVE STRATEGY SUMMARIES FOR THE BROWN FAMILY

Fig 3.7

A. The usual way - pay off the mortgage to zero, while investing as much cash as possible for 25 years at 10%.

	Debt		Tax			Net Worth After 25 Yrs.		
	Start	End	Deductions	Refunds	Time	Investments	Debt	Net Worth
Current mortgage	100,000	0	0	0	25 yrs	-	-	-
Current savings - $5,000	-	-	0	0	25 yrs	54,174	0	54,174
Monthly savings - $200	-	-	0	0	25 yrs	265,367	0	265,367
								$319,541

B. The Smith Manoeuvre way - convert the bad debt to good debt, re-borrow to invest, generate tax deductions to apply against the mortgage to increase deductible borrowing for investment, for 25 years at 10%.

	Start	End	Deductions	Refunds	Time	Investments	Debt	Net Worth
After Step I	100,000	100,000	45,200	13,560	25.00 yrs	207,103	100,000	107,103
After Step II	100,000	100,000	50,849	15,255	22.83 yrs	242,086	100,000	142,086
After Step III	100,000	100,000	65,129	19,539	19.92 yrs	335,962	100,000	235,962
After Step IV	100,000	100,000	89,485	26,845	12.67 yrs	666,541	100,000	566,541
								$566,541

C. Summary

Assuming the same starting position for each strategy regarding debt, time, investment rate of return, monthly investment amounts and current investment values, The Smith Manoeuvre has increased the future value of the Brown's net worth from $319,541 to $566,541. This is a difference of $247,000, which represents an improvement of 77%.

compared are the same, but if a lump sum reduction occurred between payments, the ratio of principal reduction to interest paid is noticeably improved in the next payment and all future payments. The mortgage amortization period is thus shortened. Shorter is better when paying off mortgages, right?

David Chilton's Method – The Wealthy Barber ©

With over 2 million copies sold, David Chilton's famous book is reportedly the most sold book in Canada, behind the Bible. It is a remarkable success story built on a premise that basic financial planning does not have to be complicated. On the investing side of financial planning, Chilton's thrust is that you should always invest 10% of your gross income for your whole working life. If you do that, you will die wealthy, and it is true.

In my 20 odd years in the financial planning business, I rarely found anyone who managed to accomplish this if they were the normal Canadian family with kids to raise, a big mortgage, a car loan, credit cards, RRSP's, and education plans to fund.

The magic of compounding is very powerful though, and you develop huge future values when you project David Chilton's assumptions by checking check box V. In Figure 3.8, you can see that Mr. Black would have $1,105,695 set aside in investments by the time his 25-year mortgage amortization period was ended, if he followed David Chilton's program – a huge sum.

The Smith Manoeuvre allows an opportunity to improve upon the results Mr. Chilton projects. Mr. Chilton advises you to invest 10% of your gross income every month, and in this case, it develops a fabulous $1.1 million fund. If Mr. Chilton is not offended, I would suggest instead he utilizes The Smith Manoeuvre, and advises Mr. Black to divert the monthly income amount as an extra payment against the first mortgage, so that Mr. Black can turn around to re-borrow the same amount of money so he can buy exactly the same amount of investments as he was planning to do. Combined with the prior, and free benefits developed already by Mr. Black who has implemented Step I through IV, Mr. Black's future value is $3,140,546 instead of $1,105,695. That's an improvement of $2,034,051 to adopt The Smith Manoeuvre instead of the Chilton Method. The incremental benefit of doing the Chilton Method

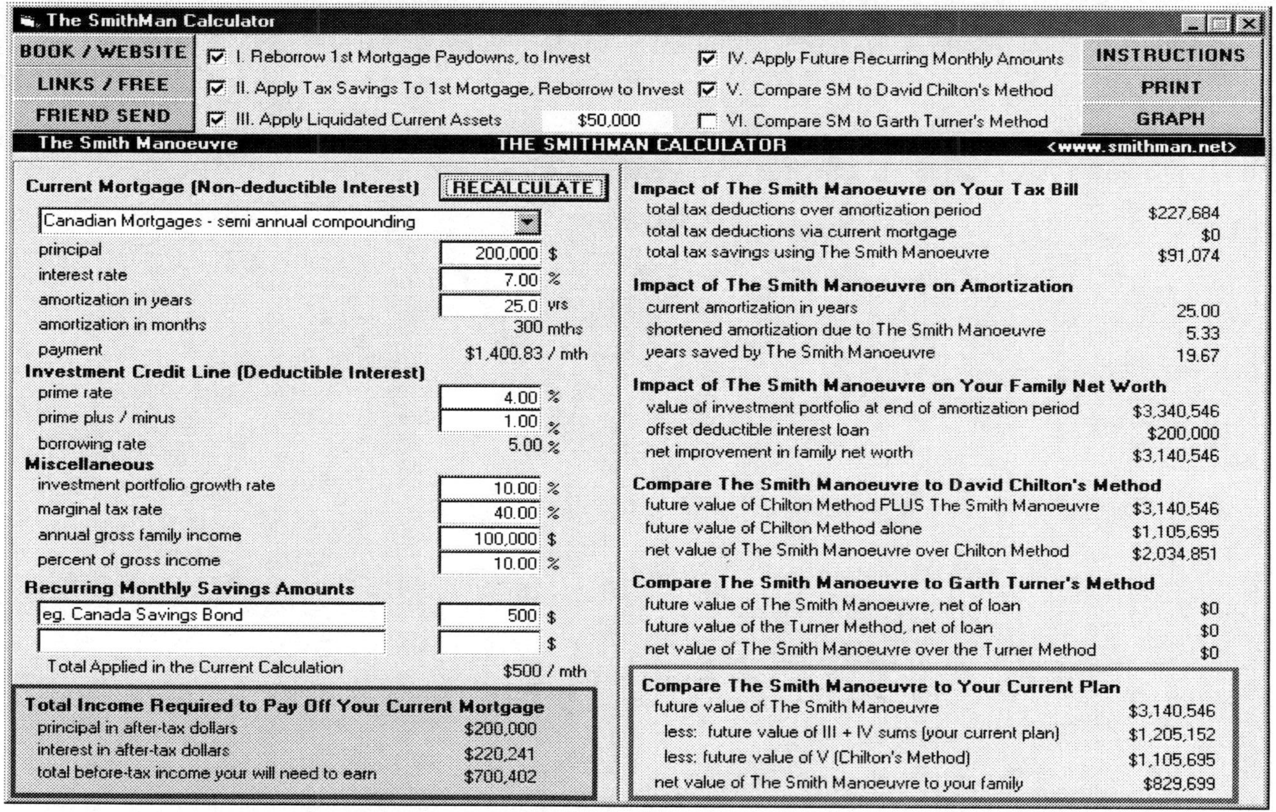

The SmithMan Calculator

BOOK / WEBSITE | LINKS / FREE | FRIEND SEND

- [x] I. Reborrow 1st Mortgage Paydowns, to Invest
- [x] II. Apply Tax Savings To 1st Mortgage, Reborrow to Invest
- [x] III. Apply Liquidated Current Assets $50,000
- [x] IV. Apply Future Recurring Monthly Amounts
- [x] V. Compare SM to David Chilton's Method
- [ ] VI. Compare SM to Garth Turner's Method

INSTRUCTIONS | PRINT | GRAPH

The Smith Manoeuvre — THE SMITHMAN CALCULATOR — <www.smithman.net>

Current Mortgage (Non-deductible Interest) RECALCULATE

Canadian Mortgages - semi annual compounding

principal	200,000	$
interest rate	7.00	%
amortization in years	25.0	yrs
amortization in months	300	mths
payment	$1,400.83	/ mth

Investment Credit Line (Deductible Interest)

prime rate	4.00	%
prime plus / minus	1.00	%
borrowing rate	5.00	%

Miscellaneous

investment portfolio growth rate	10.00	%
marginal tax rate	40.00	%
annual gross family income	100,000	$
percent of gross income	10.00	%

Recurring Monthly Savings Amounts

eg. Canada Savings Bond	500	$
		$
Total Applied in the Current Calculation	$500	/ mth

Total Income Required to Pay Off Your Current Mortgage

principal in after-tax dollars	$200,000
interest in after-tax dollars	$220,241
total before-tax income your will need to earn	$700,402

Impact of The Smith Manoeuvre on Your Tax Bill

total tax deductions over amortization period	$227,684
total tax deductions via current mortgage	$0
total tax savings using The Smith Manoeuvre	$91,074

Impact of The Smith Manoeuvre on Amortization

current amortization in years	25.00
shortened amortization due to The Smith Manoeuvre	5.33
years saved by The Smith Manoeuvre	19.67

Impact of The Smith Manoeuvre on Your Family Net Worth

value of investment portfolio at end of amortization period	$3,340,546
offset deductible interest loan	$200,000
net improvement in family net worth	$3,140,546

Compare The Smith Manoeuvre to David Chilton's Method

future value of Chilton Method PLUS The Smith Manoeuvre	$3,140,546
future value of Chilton Method alone	$1,105,695
net value of The Smith Manoeuvre over Chilton Method	$2,034,851

Compare The Smith Manoeuvre to Garth Turner's Method

future value of The Smith Manoeuvre, net of loan	$0
future value of the Turner Method, net of loan	$0
net value of The Smith Manoeuvre over the Turner Method	$0

Compare The Smith Manoeuvre to Your Current Plan

future value of The Smith Manoeuvre	$3,140,546
less: future value of III + IV sums (your current plan)	$1,205,152
less: future value of V (Chilton's Method)	$1,105,695
net value of The Smith Manoeuvre to your family	$829,699

Figure 3.8

straight up versus running the same values through the mortgage and re-borrowing can be determined by subtracting the "Net Value of The Smith Manoeuvre to Your Family" on Figure 3.8 from the equivalent number on Figure 3.5. The incremental value of The Smith Manoeuvre is therefore $829,699 minus $757,618 = $72,081. Worth doing?

Garth Turner's Method

Garth Turner is a legend in the Canadian financial planning scene as is David Chilton. Garth made his millions in real estate, became an M.P., was Minister of Revenue for Canada (The Taxman) and subsequently has written many books on RRSP investing and financial planning. In several of his books he emphasizes that Canadians should pay their house mortgage off as fast as possible, then, the day the house is free and clear, be it 10, 15 or 20 years later, you should go back to the banker and re-borrow 75% of the equity for investment purposes, and get it invested. And that's excellent advice, in my opinion, and in the opinion of thousands of Canadians who agree with this strategy. To see the results of Garth Turner's method, leave I through IV boxes checked, turn off V (Chilton) and check only box VI, (Turner). If Mr. Black followed Garth's advice, you will notice in Figure 3.9 that Mr. Black would be up by $803,215. Mr. Black's mortgage, because of the effects of The Smith Manoeuvre, is paid off in 8.08 years instead of 25 years. Following Garth's plan then, Mr. Black will re-borrow and invest $200,000 for 25 years less 8.08 years. If Mr. Black compounds $200,000 for 16.92 years, he will be up by $803,215.

But Mr. Black is up $1,962,770 million utilizing The Smith Manoeuvre, which indicates that the value of The Smith Manoeuvre for Mr. Black is over $1,159,555 better than Turner way. As good as the Turner Method is, by design it means that you defer your investing program until you have paid off your mortgage. If you manage to pay your 25-year mortgage off in 20 years, then the Turner Method means you will have to wait 20 years to start investing. Time is our friend if we have investments compounding right now, not 20 years later, or 10 years later. This rather simple fact means millions of dollars lost for Mr. Black if he follows the wrong strategy. Mr. Turner's concept is excellent and yields excellent improvements in future wealth for its users. The

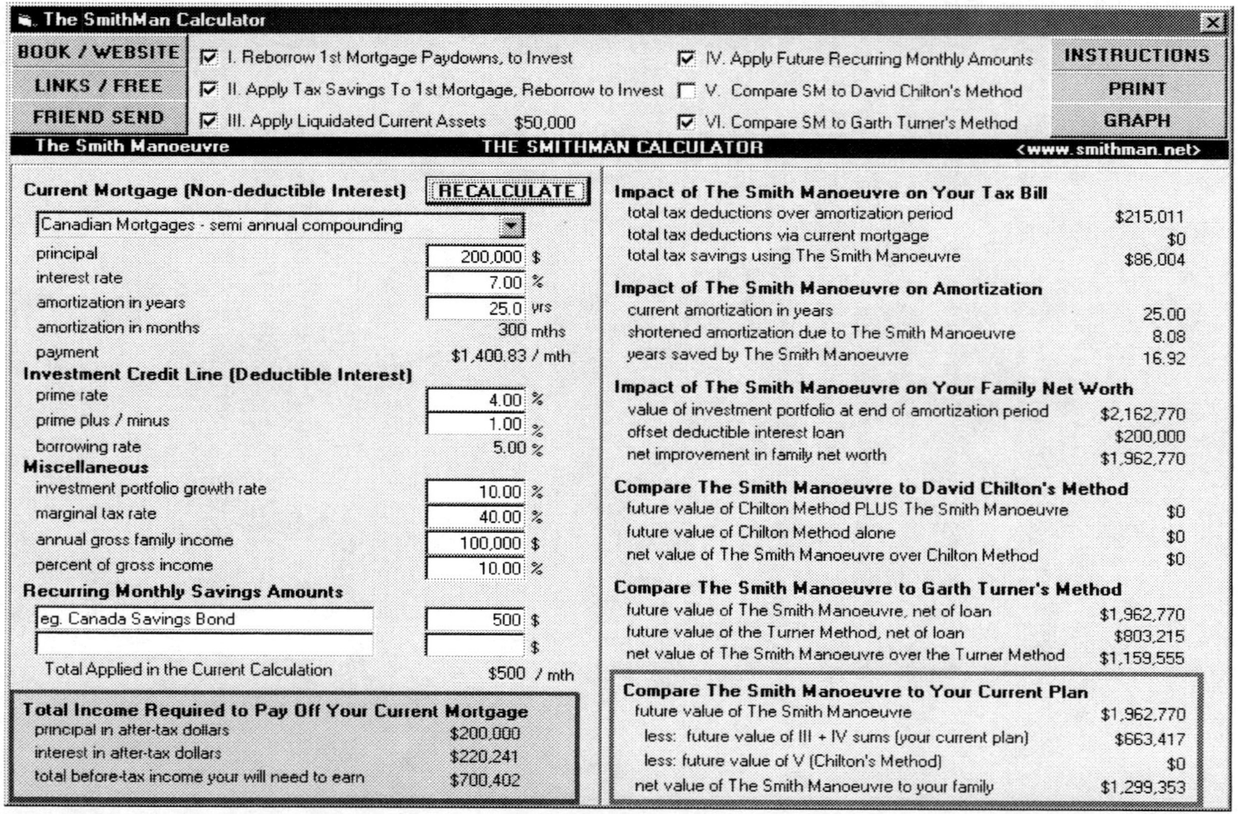

The SmithMan Calculator

BOOK / WEBSITE | LINKS / FREE | FRIEND SEND

- [x] I. Reborrow 1st Mortgage Paydowns, to Invest
- [x] II. Apply Tax Savings To 1st Mortgage, Reborrow to Invest
- [x] III. Apply Liquidated Current Assets $50,000
- [x] IV. Apply Future Recurring Monthly Amounts
- [ ] V. Compare SM to David Chilton's Method
- [x] VI. Compare SM to Garth Turner's Method

INSTRUCTIONS | PRINT | GRAPH

The Smith Manoeuvre — **THE SMITHMAN CALCULATOR** — <www.smithman.net>

Current Mortgage (Non-deductible Interest) RECALCULATE

Canadian Mortgages - semi annual compounding

principal	200,000	$
interest rate	7.00	%
amortization in years	25.0	yrs
amortization in months	300	mths
payment	$1,400.83	/ mth
Investment Credit Line (Deductible Interest)		
prime rate	4.00	%
prime plus / minus	1.00	%
borrowing rate	5.00	%
Miscellaneous		
investment portfolio growth rate	10.00	%
marginal tax rate	40.00	%
annual gross family income	100,000	$
percent of gross income	10.00	%
Recurring Monthly Savings Amounts		
eg. Canada Savings Bond	500	$
		$
Total Applied in the Current Calculation	$500	/ mth

Total Income Required to Pay Off Your Current Mortgage	
principal in after-tax dollars	$200,000
interest in after-tax dollars	$220,241
total before-tax income your will need to earn	$700,402

Impact of The Smith Manoeuvre on Your Tax Bill	
total tax deductions over amortization period	$215,011
total tax deductions via current mortgage	$0
total tax savings using The Smith Manoeuvre	$86,004
Impact of The Smith Manoeuvre on Amortization	
current amortization in years	25.00
shortened amortization due to The Smith Manoeuvre	8.08
years saved by The Smith Manoeuvre	16.92
Impact of The Smith Manoeuvre on Your Family Net Worth	
value of investment portfolio at end of amortization period	$2,162,770
offset deductible interest loan	$200,000
net improvement in family net worth	$1,962,770
Compare The Smith Manoeuvre to David Chilton's Method	
future value of Chilton Method PLUS The Smith Manoeuvre	$0
future value of Chilton Method alone	$0
net value of The Smith Manoeuvre over Chilton Method	$0
Compare The Smith Manoeuvre to Garth Turner's Method	
future value of The Smith Manoeuvre, net of loan	$1,962,770
future value of the Turner Method, net of loan	$803,215
net value of The Smith Manoeuvre over the Turner Method	$1,159,555

Compare The Smith Manoeuvre to Your Current Plan	
future value of The Smith Manoeuvre	$1,962,770
less: future value of III + IV sums (your current plan)	$663,417
less: future value of V (Chilton's Method)	$0
net value of The Smith Manoeuvre to your family	$1,299,353

Figure 2.9

Smith Manoeuvre simply makes a good idea even better.

So congratulations to Mr. Turner and Mr. Chilton for the wonderful improvements they have generated for thousands of Canadians. If they embrace The Smith Manoeuvre, their gift will be grandly enhanced.

What About Other Non-Deductible Loans?

Your objective should be to convert all types of non-deductible debt to deductible debt. For instance, if you have a $30,000 loan for the family car, you are usually paying a goodly sum of non-deductible interest each time you make your car payment. The mechanics of converting the bad debt to good debt is similar to what you have seen in these prior pages. I call it The Mini Smith Manoeuvre.

Executing The Mini Smith Manoeuvre

Step 1

Speak with the loans manager of the bank that holds your car loan.

Step 2

Explain that your objective is to convert your non-deductible interest car loan to a deductible interest creditline for investment purposes. If your car loan is for $30,000, your plan is to open an investment creditline of $30,000. If your credit is good enough, you will be granted the creditline on an unsecured basis.

Step 3

If the banker requests security, offer the car. But the car is already security for the original outstanding car loan. That's ok, because you can agree that the two loan totals added together will not rise about $30,000. For example, you agree that if you want to borrow $5,000 to invest, you will not be able to do so until you have reduced the car loan by $5,000. In this arrangement the banker feels safe, and justified in using the car as security for both loans, because added together, the total indebtedness is only $30,000 or less, never more.

Step 4

If the banker is still leery, offer the security of the car loan *plus* the investments you intend to purchase. This should do it – he is now double secured (be sure to write in that when the conversion is complete your securities will be released as collateral, leaving only the car as security).

Step 5

If your banker has not cooperated by now, advise him you are going shopping. A few phone calls will provide you names of bankers who are happy to provide this mini version of The Smith Manoeuvre. Remember, it's no skin off a banker's nose to give you this service.

1. You are not increasing your debt; you are converting if from the bad kind to the good kind.

2. You are offering the bank the same or better security.

3. You will have additional assets/wealth that neither you nor the banker contemplated before you read this book. If you are better off, the bank's loan with you is safer. He likes that.

4. The cash benefits you begin receiving now are not paid by the banker, they are paid by the taxman. *This is an extra, tax-free income* for your family.

5. Your car loan is your liability, but it is the bank's asset. Every day, as millions of Canadians make their car payments, the assets of the banks are declining. You are offering your banker a solution – give you The Mini Smith Manoeuvre, and for at least a few years, your loan, his asset, will stay level while you engineer the conversion of your debt from the bad kind to the good kind. And if you like the way The Mini Smith Manoeuvre is improving your financial well being, he might just end up happily still holding your loan when finally you exit this world at age 130. Why would you ever pay off this beautiful tax-deductible interest loan? But that's your

decision to make, at a later date, certainly no sooner than the time it takes to make all that interest into on-going tax deductions.

The Mini Smith Manoeuvre is what you use to convert those miscellaneous non-deductible loans into juicy tax deductions.

If you have a house mortgage and one or two other non-deductible interest loans such as car loans, credit card debt, consolidation loans and the like, it is usually best to rank order them in their cost to you, and apply The Mini Smith Manoeuvre against your worst loan first, converting them one after the other until you are done. High interest non-deductible loans hurt you most while they are still non-deductible. The reverse is true if you turn those bad loans into good loans.

So take some time to map out your work plan, then get at it so you can bring these financial savings home for your family to enjoy.

4

WEALTH ACCUMULATION

Saving vs. Investing

In the Black's case, the accumulation of savings has occurred because prior to now they have been diverting 6% of their gross income each month to buy CSB's, term deposits and GIC's. These are savings systems as opposed to investment systems. The Blacks are lending their hard earned after-tax dollars to government or big businesses, such as the banks. In return they earn a very low rate of interest, and then at the end of the year, whatever small amount they did earn is taxed at 40%. So a bad investment is made worse.

On the other hand, these savings vehicles are safe. Even though the government is broke, they can always raise your taxes to get enough money from you, to give you back the small percentage they need to give you as your interest, then at the end of the year they will tax you at 40% on what they gave you for interest, which they got from you in taxes. So you are "safe"... safely losing money, that is.

Let Me Give You an Example.

There is a wonderful company called Andex in Windsor, Ontario that makes all kinds of charts comparing the performances of the stock markets against the money markets, including 5 year GIC's, long term bonds, and 90 day Canada T-Bills (visit them at *www.andexcharts.com*).

As of the middle of 2001, the 51-year history of Canada T-Bills showed an average annual rate of return of 6.3% per year. At 40% tax, the after-tax return would be 3.8% per year. Pretty poor. But wait. The annual average inflation rate for those same 51 years stands at 4.1%. Take inflation off of your 3.8% after tax return, and you will see that yes, you are safe. You are safely losing ground. To be fair, a 5-year GIC, after tax and after inflation would leave you with a positive return of ½ of 1 percent. Wow.

Part of the problem is that government and large institutions don't pay much interest, but another part of the problem is that even that small amount of interest is fully taxed every year by the wasteful, greedy and corrupt federal government.

If these debt style instruments are losing money, what should you invest in?

Investing in Real Estate

You could buy investment real estate, which might be better than investing in debt instruments. Might be.

Many excellent business writers point to three pressures on real estate as an investment class:

1. It is not a very liquid investment

2. Prices for houses across much of Canada are generally too high such that it is difficult to consistently earn decent profit margins when operating them as rentals. This is because rents traditionally do not rise in direct proportion to the increase in the capital cost of the property. A $100,000 revenue house in 1980 might have brought in $800 per month. Now that the rental has doubled in value to $200,000, it hurts that the rental house only commands $1,200 in rent. The capital tied up has doubled, but the rent income has only gone up 50%.

3. It is broadly forecast by demographers and financial experts such as Garth Turner that as the baby boomers start to retire, some will downsize. It does not take too much of a surplus in any one price band to reduce prices across the board. In addition, the number of homebuyers coming on stream is a much smaller cohort than the cohort that is getting ready to retire. This translates to less than normal demand. This double negative does not bode well for single-family residential housing once the baby boomers start to retire "en bloc".

If housing and debt investments are marginal, what is left?

Despite the shock of the dot com bust and the mess of crooked companies currently getting caught in their tawdry escapades, it looks as though investment in equities is still the best bet for the bulk of your investing. As I write this in the summer of 2002, the markets have been dipping and there is a whiff of panic in the air.

It's not much fun sometimes, but if we know that doing nothing is a losing proposition, and if we know debt instruments are not much better than breakeven, and if we do comprehend the realities that will likely come to real estate because of the laws of supply and demand, then perhaps it's equities by default.

While equities are down as I write, they have always done well if you stay in and ignore the volatility. If you have no plans to sell your house, then it tends to matter little to you if house prices are dropping or rising – you don't pay much attention. We should learn to do the same with equity investments.

It is interesting to use the Andex Charts to make comparisons of equities similar to the comparisons I made for debt instruments.

Over the same 51 years, the TSE has averaged an annual return of 10.7%. In the best light, assuming the earnings for all those years were reinvested capital gains, then today's figure would be 10.7% for both before-tax and after-tax considerations because you would pay no tax until the securities were sold. You would still subtract inflation of 4.1% to yield 6.6%, which is rather excellent.

While it is possible to own 100% tax efficient equities as in the prior example, in reality, most portfolios will have some taxation occurring each year. There is no doubt that you would bet on equities over debt investments on most any day of the year while in your working years. As we get older we may feel we have to take less return in order to increase the safety of our capital.

Some will say that equities are too volatile, but the scenario we paint for users of The Smith Manoeuvre is that they should invest in equities, they should be broadly diversified in different asset classes, they should lean to blue chip, they should purchase on a dollar-cost-averaging basis and therefore avoid trying to be market timers. At least until they have the ability to predict the future.

Volatility does not hurt us if we are not trying to time the market. The Andex Charts show that in no decade since 1950 has the ten-year average dropped below 10% per year for the TSE.

The equivalent 51-year performance for the Standard and Poor index in the USA is 13.6%, which is 22% better than Canada's stock market performance. This is evidence to further support the common sense notion that we should be investing in several countries of the world if we want to increase returns and decrease risk.

What's Important Here?

Regardless of whether you agree about what kind of investing is best for you, it should be noted that your net worth will improve in large amounts when you liquidate current assets, use the proceeds to over-pay your mortgage, then borrow back to repurchase the assets you sold, or better ones. (Be aware that you can't sell and repurchase the *identical* asset within 30 days of the sale.) Ask your financial planner or accountant to explain the superficial loss rules to you.

What About RRSP's?

The mathematics around The Smith Manoeuvre and RRSP's is complicated by the fact that RRSP's grow tax-free and also yield tax deductions. They are a fabulous invention and very powerful investment vehicles for Canadians. Garth Turner has written several first class books on this topic that you should read. (Order these books from Garth's excellent website *www.garth.ca*.) Garth knows of what he speaks because he made millions from real estate and now buys equities. He follows his own advice. He is also one of Canada's former cabinet ministers as Minister of Revenue. He was the taxman.

RRSP's and their place in The Smith Manoeuvre will be the subject of an update to this book. Watch the website (*www.smithman.net*) for news on this front.

Early indications are that your net worth will improve significantly if you sell your existing RRSP, bring the cash out and pay the tax now, use the residue to pay down your first and re-borrow to invest *outside* the RRSP.

It looks like the incremental improvement of net worth because of the reduction of the mortgage *now,* beats leaving an RRSP to grow on a tax-deferred basis. This up-front advantage regarding the mortgage, when combined with the after-tax considerations at the end of the amortization period, makes The Smith Manoeuvre more powerful than an RRSP.

If it's true that you should cash in your RRSP to increment The Smith Manoeuvre, it follows that you should also divert current and future RRSP purchases against your first mortgage. The RRSP purchase would only be diverted until the first mortgage was paid off. Once you are rid of your first mortgage, the next best use of cash flow would be to return to buying maximum RRSP's.

The comparison of before-tax and after-tax incomes is an important way to analyze correctly the impact of financial decisions we need to make in life. A very important booklet on this subject *Dispelling the Myths of Borrowing to Invest* has been written by one of Canada's up and coming financial gurus, Talbot Stevens. Read about him, and order his book via his website at *www.talbotstevens.com*.

In summary, the Plain Jane Smith Manoeuvre, Step I and II will give you free new money from the tax department, which will be used to pay down your first mortgage faster so you can borrow back to invest faster. Sooner is better when it comes to paying off your mortgage. Sooner is also better when you want your investments to maximize their compounding years. Ask Einstein.

Step III and Step IV represent the Enhanced Plain Jane Smith Manoeuvre. In Step III, you will be able to calculate the financial advantage of selling current assets using the proceeds to reduce your first mortgage, then using your newly generated home equity to borrow back money to repurchase the assets you sold, or better assets. Step IV diverts monthly sums against your mortgage as extra monthly over-payments that you may be paying now to buy CSB's term deposits, GIC's, mutual funds or stocks and bonds. You will be able to calculate the effect of these strategies using THE SMITHMAN CALCULATOR available at *www.smithman.net*.

Finally, it must be apparent that any funds you turn up as bonuses, gifts, inheritances, garage sales, etc., will benefit you best of all if you always use them to reduce your first mortgage so that you can borrow back the money immediately so you can buy appreciating assets. And enjoy even more free tax refunds.

Manulife has figured this out and you should look at one of their newer mortgage products, Manulife One, which is a great program. It really sings when combined with the horsepower of The Smith Manoeuvre.

Now that you have used THE SMITHMAN CALCULATOR to analyze and compare your mortgage and investment strategies, it is time to round out our understanding about interest expense.

5

INTEREST EXPENSE

Deductible versus Non-Deductible Interest

In some countries such as the United States, most loan interest paid by a taxpayer may be deducted from other income at tax-filing time regardless of what purpose the money was borrowed for in the first place. This generates a tax refund cheque to the favour of the American taxpayer.

In Canada, the tax department is not so generous. Interest paid on money borrowed to buy the family car, vacations, cottages, credit card consolidation and "general consumption" cannot be deducted from other income for purposes of calculating income tax. No tax refund cheque for the Canadian taxpayer.

More importantly, interest on the largest loan many Canadians will ever take out, their house mortgage, is also not tax deductible. This is a huge disadvantage to Canadians.

How Huge?

If a Canadian family and an American family have both taken out a $200,000 mortgage with a 25 year amortization and 7% interest, each family will have to repay the $200,000 principal amount borrowed, plus approximately an additional $220,000 in interest expense. This totals about $420,000.

The American may deduct the $220,000 interest expense from his other income, and at a 40% tax rate, the American will receive an $88,000 tax refund over the life of the mortgage. Assume he invests his tax refunds and earns 10% per year for 25 years, and you will begin to understand how important it is to make interest tax deductible whenever you can. That's because the invested tax refunds will generate about $700,000 free, for our American friend.

The Canadian has to pay back the full $420,000 too, but with no tax refunds, and therefore no investments are possible. Worse than that, the full $420,000 for our disadvantaged Canadian will be paid with after-tax dollars. At the 40% tax bracket that means our hapless citizen will have to earn $700,000, pay income tax at 40%, which is $280,000, in order to be able to have $420,000 with which to pay the principal and interest on his tiny $200,000 mortgage loan. It must be coming clear to the reader that it is critical to find a way to convert your mortgage interest into a tax deduction if you live in Canada. Want to know what your equivalent numbers are? They are calculated for you automatically as a function of the software contained in THE SMITHMAN CALCULATOR.

To be fair, it should be pointed out that in Canada, we enjoy tax-free capital gains if we make a profit when we sell our home. In the States, the capital gains that might occur upon sale of the principal residence are taxed. These are modest offsets - if you could choose between deductible interest or tax free capital gains, you would take deductible interest.

If you employ The Smith Manoeuvre, you will have the benefit of deductible interest as well as no capital gains tax upon the sale of your home, the best tax advantages of both countries. Suddenly, Canadians utilizing The Smith Manoeuvre will have even larger financial advantages than their American cousins.

The fact that our American friends can deduct most of their mortgage interest when we can't goes some distance to explain why their standard of living is higher than ours in Canada.

A $200,000 house mortgage at 7% interest costs approximately $13,700 in interest during the first year, whether you live in Canada or the United States. The difference is that the American can claim the interest as deductible and, at a 40% marginal tax rate, he would receive a tax refund of $13,700 x .40 = $5,480. You, as a Canadian, may claim no tax refund. Unless you know how to do The Smith Manoeuvre.

The Canada Customs and Revenue Agency (CCRA) is very strict about claims for deductibility of interest. This topic bears repeating. The basic test for deductibility revolves around the answer to the question *'to what purpose did you put the money that you borrowed?'* If you borrowed to buy the family car, to take a vacation, to buy a cottage or your principal residence, then you may not claim the interest on the loan as a tax deduction. On the other hand, if you borrowed the money to invest, with a reasonable expectation of earning income from your investment, you may deduct the interest.

Interest and dividends from investments are acceptable forms of earned income for purposes of determining deductible interest claims, but capital gains are not. In the case of borrowing to invest in mutual funds and stock, the CCRA has so far allowed the interest to be deductible even in the cases where a portion of the gain is likely to be capital gains. Your financial planner or your accountant will counsel you on this matter if he feels you are exposed in any way.

Some Canadians assume that if their house is the bank's security for a loan, then the interest is not tax deductible. This is important --- the security offered for a loan has nothing to do with whether the interest expense is deductible. The main test is – *'what did you do with the money that you borrowed?'*

Some Canadians assume that conventional loans with blended payments that include both an interest and a principal reduction component are, by their nature, in the non-deductible category. This is also not true. Again, the type of loan, whether interest-only or blended payments, whether secured by your home or not, does not impact whether the interest is deductible. What matters is, *'to what purpose did you put the money that you borrowed?'*

The Next Time you Borrow

If the foregoing is making sense to you, it might be apparent that most Canadians and their bankers are getting their borrowing mechanics exactly backwards.

Imagine that a hard working and bright young lady has scrimped and saved to put together $30,000 of capital to invest in a business. Unfortunately, just as she is ready to buy her new business, her car blows up, and it becomes obvious that she also needs to borrow another $30,000 for a new family car. So she visits her friendly bank manager and asks for a $30,000 loan.

The bank manager is impressed. Usually people are coming to borrow money when they have no money, but this ambitious lady has $30,000 of her own. She looks like a good risk to him, so he smiles a big smile and says, "sit right down and I will write you up a car loan for $30,000."

And everybody is happy. Our heroine went in for a $30,000 loan and got it. The banker has made a low risk loan to a motivated young business lady. The carmaker has sold another car. And in the background, the taxman is smiling too because the way the loan was written up, the interest expense will not be tax deductible.

The loan was made backwards. A common but large mistake.

Our new business lady can be forgiven for making the mistake of asking for "a loan" instead of "an *investment* loan" because she was not taught the crucial difference between deductible interest (good interest) and non-deductible interest (bad interest) in her public school. Unless she subsequently went to business school, the odds are that she was not taught the difference at university or college either. Her parents and her relatives, her friends and her co-workers, plus her neighbours to the front, behind and next-door are likely all doing it wrong as well. They tend to make poor teachers regarding things financial. That's one reason financial planners were invented. If you don't have one you should consider getting one.

Very few Canadians understand the importance of differentiating between good debt and bad debt. In fact, very few Canadians know much about personal financial planning. It is written elsewhere that most Canadians spent more time last night watching TV than they have spent in their entire life learning about personal financial planning.

If I were the King of Canada, I would, as one of my first acts, decree that every year, starting with Grade One, part of the curriculum would be devoted to personal financial planning. The payoff for the students, and the resultant payoff for Canada would be immense. Canadians would learn how to take care of their own financial well being rather than depending on failing government retirement programs.

But what about the banker?

Does the banker understand how important this distinction between good debt and bad debt really is? What should the banker have done when this woman came in to see him for her loan?

Instead of selling her a non-deductible interest loan for a car, he should instead have sold her a deductible-interest loan so she could invest the borrowed money into her new business. That simple act, at no disadvantage to the bank, would have made the customer's interest expense a tax deduction.

He either knew, or should have known, that the difference to his customer was very important.

If the loan interest rate was 6%, then the first year interest expense on the $30,000 loan would be about $1,800 dollars, regardless of whether the loan was for investment in her business or for the car. But if the loan was for the business, the $1,800 interest expense would be tax deductible. At the 40% tax bracket, our young entrepreneur would receive a $720 tax refund cheque, no charge, a gift, free, gratis, from the tax department.

That's a nice reward for simply writing up a loan one-way versus the other way. But there's more. Next year there will be another tax refund cheque, also free. And the year after that. In fact, if the loan was established as an interest-only loan, our business lady could still be getting free tax refund cheques for $720 every year until she retired at age 130.

If the bank manager knew, or should have known, that he could have provided a tax refund of such a magnitude to his customer simply by counseling her to borrow for the business purpose so she could use her own tax-paid funds to buy her car, and if the amount of interest the bank was getting for either type of loan was identical, why did he sell her the wrong loan?

You might guess that the bank would prefer to take the loan security of a car over the loan security of a new business, which is probably true. But nothing precludes the banker from taking the security of the car for the investment loan. The customer would be indifferent. If the banker had any reservations about the loan, he could even request the security of both the car and the new business. So the security for the loan is not the reason that the banker did not do this no-cost favour for the customer.

Perhaps the reason is simply because banks have always done it that way. This simply shows that the educated borrower has a better chance for success in this life than does the uneducated borrower.

Conspiracy theorists will say that the Grey People in Government are colluding with the Grey People in the Banking Industry to keep the minions ignorant about the power of deductible interest.

By paying attention to the simple rule that you use borrowed money to make your investments, and you use your own tax-paid funds to buy your life style such as food, clothing, vacations, cars, toys, cottages and your home, you will be enormously ahead of your friends, neighbours and co-workers, as measured by your net worth.

The Least Known Strategy

As you are learning, The Smith Manoeuvre is going to generate thousands of dollars of free tax deductions for thousands of Canadians, including you. The Smith Manoeuvre gains its power to perform by amalgamating several separate strategies with synergistic effects.

During my early days researching mortgages, banking, taxation and other exciting matters, I tripped into Section 20(c) of The Tax Act of Canada. In that dimly lit section of that dimly lit book, I read the part that says that if the interest on your loan is deductible, then so is the interest-on-the-interest the next month, and so on. *The compounding interest on a tax-deductible loan is itself deductible.*

By itself, that doesn't sound too earthshaking. Over many months I kept going back to that piece of news because I had a niggle. I was attracted to that item, but not sure why.

I don't remember for sure when it happened, but one day a light went on and I suddenly realized that I should not be letting my clients pay the interest monthly on their deductible interest investment loans that were growing each month as their first mortgage was melting towards zero.

At least not until the first mortgage was extinguished.

The rationale? If the rule is that you use your own cash to pay off bad loans, such as your house mortgage and you borrow for investments so that you generate tax-deductible interest expense, then it follows that you should not use your cash to reduce deductible loans or pay interest on them. Instead of paying the interest on the tax-deductible loan, use your cash to make an extra payment against your house mortgage. What will the bank say when you don't pay the interest expense on your investment loan? It will be something like "what about the interest you owe us on this investment loan?"

You are ready with the answer, which my clients have been providing for nearly 20 years now – "please, sir, please capitalize the interest expense this month." And the banker does, if he is operating The Smith Manoeuvre for you.

Notice that your total debt did not change. The bad loan went down by the same amount the good loan increased.

Capitalization is a financial term that in this case simply means, calculate the interest on a loan, and then, if you can't pay the interest, just increase the principal amount of the loan by the amount of the unpaid interest.

This is normally not too good for borrowers or for lenders. The borrower's loan gets bigger each month, on a compounding basis. The banker has a non-performing loan. So why do it?

The underlying concept of The Smith Manoeuvre is that it is good to convert bad debt to good debt. It's good to do the debt conversion to generate free tax refund cheques in large amounts each year for the rest of your life. If it's good to convert the debt, then sooner is better than later. The best of all worlds would be to do the conversion in one day, and it has been done. Most people can't do it that fast. Anything we can do to speed up the time it takes to convert the bad debt to good debt is good for us. This is because we get to the maximum tax refund cheques sooner. This let's us invest sooner, and when it comes to investing, time is our friend.

And this is the diamond in the rough: The Smith Manoeuvre is converting your debt from the bad kind (where compounding interest is killing you while simultaneously it makes the bank wealthy) to the good kind of debt (which is debt that provides you the cash to buy assets that will compound their value year after year, to your benefit).

Don't worry about the banks. They get wealthy in either scenario. As you will discover in Chapter 7, it is fortunate for you that the banks are indifferent as to whether your debt with them is bad debt or good debt.

Here is another gem I uncovered. While I was excited at my discovery, I admit to initial concern about the reaction of the tax department if I was claiming tax deductions for interest that I didn't actually pay from my wallet. It turns out, however, that the tax department allows you the tax deduction whether you pay your interest expense with cash or borrowed money. To the tax department, it is satisfactory that you have borrowed the money from the bank to pay the interest you owe the bank, which is what has happened when you capitalized the interest on the original loan.

The bank simply totals the amount of interest they earned on your deductible interest investment loan for the whole year. Whether you paid it with cash (don't – at least until your first mortgage is paid off) or whether you borrowed it from them by capitalizing, that total interest amount for the year is your tax deduction. When you report that number on your tax return you will subsequently receive a very welcome tax refund cheque, free.

My Bank Doesn't Want to Capitalize

They probably won't in the early days ahead. But a financial revolution has been taking place. Partly because of foreign competition but mostly because ordinary people are using the Internet to get educated, things are changing rapidly. So the big banks may initially be reluctant to capitalize for you, but as more people like you request these services, they will begin to co-operate. This is because they will start losing their mortgages to other banks and credit unions like VanCity and Coast Capital. They will eventually come around. It is called competition and free enterprise. The market is very powerful. If you are rejected by your bank for capitalization privileges, shop around for other more caring institutions, such as the credit unions. In the alternative, retain a financial planner who offers assistance with The Smith Manoeuvre.

If you and your planner are unable to find any institution in your area that will capitalize, implement The Smith Manoeuvre without the capitalization feature. You will be able to enjoy capitalization later because sooner or later, this service will undoubtedly be common practice in your locale.

If you and your advisor are determined, you can effect capitalization in the following manner. This move requires two banks or two accounts at the same bank. This is a guerrilla style personal financing strategy.

1. Set up standard Smith Manoeuvre banking arrangements at a bank or credit union.
2. If the institution refuses to offer capitalization services, open a small creditline at the same bank or a different bank, for, say, $5,000.
3. When your deductible interest creditline statement arrives indicating you owe, say, $200 interest for the month, ask the bank to capitalize the interest for you.
4. If they won't, borrow $200 from your $5,000 creditline at the same bank or a different bank and pay the interest expense.
5. Do this every month until you have borrowed, say, $4,000 of interest from the $5,000 creditline.

6. Now borrow $4,000 from your main deductible interest creditline and pay the $5,000 creditline back down to zero and start again.
7. The interest on both the $5,000 creditline and your main investment line is tax deductible because proceeds were transferred back and forth between two credit facilities that were themselves for investment purposes or for paying tax-deductible interest. As per section 20(c), compounding interest on deductible loans is itself, deductible.
8. It is this knowledge that the banks have but don't explain to ordinary people that will lead them to agree that they might as well just offer capitalization services. This is because I've shown you how to do it with or without their help.

Caution: You must never use either of these deductible interest investment lines to purchase anything that is not an investment, as it will disqualify your claim for deductible interest.

If you discover a mistake, reverse the error, preferably with the help of a planner, including the reversal of any and all compound interest on the tainted capital. Document the account activity in detail and keep copies of the applicable cheques and bank statements for the review of the taxman who will almost certainly reassess you if your records are not in order. And that's fair enough, in my opinion.

In the same vein, you need to realize that if you purchase an investment with borrowed money and claim the interest as a tax deduction, the CCRA is very strict on the rule that that asset always be in your possession if you continue to claim the interest deduction. No asset, no deduction, unless you sell an asset and immediately repurchase a new qualifying asset to take its place. It is not as simple as this, so once more you are advised to get help from your planner who is quite aware of what precautions you need to take to stay onside with Mr. Taxman.

One last caution. Some planners (poor planners) in the past have recommended that you borrow to buy an asset, claim the deductible interest, then contribute the asset to the RRSP to claim another tax benefit. Just so you know, the tax department assumes you have sold that asset the moment you put it into the RRSP, and as previously indicated, that portion of the loan invested in the transferred asset will have its applicable interest expense disqualified from being deductible from that moment forward.

You may transfer assets that were purchased with borrowed money to an RRSP but the interest expense will cease to be deductible. Keep great records, just in case.

This chapter will be somewhat mystifying to some readers no doubt. If this were easy, everybody would already be doing it. So, while it may be a bit daunting for some, the hope is that you will persevere to get a basic grounding in why it is important for you to convert your bad debt to good debt now rather than later.

You now understand that good debt is much, much better for you than bad debt. Your problem seems insurmountable because you already have a lot of debt in your house mortgage and it's the bad kind.

Is it too late for you?

6

IMPLEMENTATION

The Smith Manoeuvre is egalitarian. It is going to provide a service to anyone in Canada who has a conventional mortgage on his or her home, with some modest exceptions. Ordinary Canadians using The Smith Manoeuvre will be able to deduct the interest expense of their mortgages, a privilege ordinarily reserved for the wealthy, who can afford high priced lawyers and accountants to show them how it's done.

That being said, there are some mortgages that will be delayed in their implementation of The Smith Manoeuvre. It will be too soon for you if you have less than 25% equity in your home. You will find the financial institutions unenthusiastic if you have a high-ratio mortgage (over 75% of home value). You may find resistance if you are a farm or hobby farm. You may also find the lending value reduced to a maximum of 60% of value if you are not inside "town limits".

There are strategies to follow if you need to get down to the 75% level.

1. Sell some assets and apply the proceeds against the mortgage.
2. Borrow enough to pay the first mortgage down to the 75% level. The banker you are approaching to set up The Smith Manoeuvre will usually be happy to lend you funds on a secured or unsecured basis if you are then going to pay down your first mortgage with the proceeds. This "borrowing from Peter to pay Paul" is usually a bad scene, but the banker is apt to feel differently if the new funds allow you to start up The Smith Manoeuvre program.

You may also be delayed if you currently have more than one mortgage on your property. A good financial planner or an interested and motivated banker will usually be able to make it work as long as the two mortgages (or even three) don't exceed 75% of the value of the home. In fact, the real live client case to follow had two prior mortgages. It was the VanCity manager who suggested a great solution.

The Whites Do The Smith Manoeuvre

The first thing to realize is that banks or credit unions offering The Smith Manoeuvre services will offer to set up your readvanceable second mortgage such that it "wraps around" your existing first mortgage at another institution. It is not a requirement that you give up your relationship with your current bank. You have three options:

1. Arrange with your current banker to have him provide the readvanceable second mortgage facility.
2. Leave your first mortgage where it is and shop other institutions for the readvanceable second mortgage.
3. Shop other institutions for a package deal that pays out your current first mortgage and consolidates your financing requirements.

Imagine it as an amoeba hunting for food. The amoeba surrounds its victim and proceeds to suck the life out of it until there is nothing but a shell left. VanCity does the same. With my assistance, they sneak up on your Royal Bank first mortgage and surround it with their second readvanceable.

They do all they can to encourage you to pay the Royal's first mortgage rapidly, which is your objective in any event. For every dollar you reduce the Royal Bank mortgage, VanCity gets to lend one dollar back to you to invest. Complacency dominates as the 25-year asset at the Royal disappears in a few years or even months, and ends up instead, in the gut of VanCity. The financial amoeba has eaten the Royal Bank's lunch. But that's business.

Since the lifeblood of the banks is residential mortgages, so you can bet that the banks will respond in kind. They will all start offering The Smith Manoeuvre facilities, and they will all start offering the perks of appraisal fees and legal fees in order to match the likes of Manulife Bank who are onto a good thing with their Manulife One program. All this is good for you, the taxed to death consumer, so get out there and try a few different institutions on to see what they can do to help set up your Smith Manoeuvre.

Perhaps the easiest way to illustrate the steps you will take to establish The Smith Manoeuvre for your family is to utilize the documents exchanged with VanCity in a real live case.

Following are the pertinent rounded statistics on real live clients whom we will call Jim and

Brenda White. This young couple work hard in the hospitality industry – Jim is a chef and Brenda is a receptionist. I set them up in The Smith Manoeuvre a year ago, in the summer of 2001.

50,000	joint income
184,000	appraised house value
129,000	total of 1st and 2nd BNS mortgages
88,000	term deposits, GIC's, currency
12,000	Mazda truck – 1994
162,000	net worth

On June 4th, I faxed a financing proposal to Greg Duncan at VanCity on behalf of the Whites (Figures 6.1.1 and 6.1.2). On June 7th, Greg Duncan faxed back his approval (Figure 6.2). He included a suggestion that the Whites would be further ahead to let VanCity payout both Bank of Nova Scotia (BNS) mortgages, even with a prepayment penalty to the BNS. And he was correct.

The Whites subsequently began investing by automatic withdrawal from their VanCity deductible investment creditline at the rate of $800 per month, and have not missed a month since.

The figure of $800 represents the approximate monthly reduction of the principal of the first

Suite 104
7851 East Saanich Road
Saanichton, B.C.
V8M 2B4

Affiliated Companies
KittyHawk Securities Ltd.
KittyHawk Consulting Inc.
Granville West Capital Corp.

Smith Consulting Group Ltd.

June 4, 2001

VanCity
3055A Scott Street
Victoria, B.C. V8R 4J9

By Fax: 595-5133

Attention: Mr. Greg Duncan & Ms. Bev Shingles

Dear Greg & Bev,

is the chef at and runs the front desk at the They wish to set up the Smith Manoeuvre in order to convert their mortgage to tax deductible interest.

<u>Income</u>

	$28,704
	21,696
	$50,400

<u>Background</u>

The bought a house a year ago and assumed the vendors 6.05% BNS first and took a $44,700 BNS second. They made a $45,000 down payment, and have been overpaying the mortgages ever since. They have an unused $6,000 BNS credit line, and a VISA card that they payout each month. They have no debt other than the two mortgages.

The term of the BNS first matured today, and at our suggestion, the have renewed it as an open mortgage. (The BNS 2nd has another 2 years on its term.)

<u>Values</u>

				Actual
		$180,000	estimated value	184,000 appraisal.
	x .75%	135,000	lending value	x.75 138,000 lending value
	88,900		BNS 1st	
	40,000		BNS 2nd	
less:	$128,900	128,900	prior mortgages	− 126,865 BNS
		$ 6,100	available credit	$11,135 avail credit
				+25 K line

<u>Re-Financing</u>

Subject to confirmation of the appraisal value, our request is that VanCity supply a readvanceable mortgage for $135,000 being 75% of the property value, plus a $25,000 unsecured line of credit.

Figure 6.1.1

Use of Proceeds

The readvanceable will be used to payout the current BNS open first mortgage. The current BNS second mortgage will automatically move into first position.

The readvanceable will be set up in two segments. Segment A will be an open line of credit, non-deductible, which will be paid down very rapidly, and will be the amount needed to pay out the BNS first.

Segment B will be the deductible interest credit line to be used for investment purposes only, and will capitalize the interest monthly.

The BNS $6,000 credit line will be maintained as an unused emergency account.

The $25,000 unsecured credit line will be used to purchase Please arrange servicing of this credit line at interest only, to be paid automatically each month from Segment B of the readvanceable.

Debt Service Ratio

$ 465	$ 6,000	BNS C/L, if drawn	p+1.5
4,236	40,000	BNS second mortgage, $353/mth	7.45%
1,408		property tax	
6,445	88,900	VanCity - Segment A readvanceable	p+1
442	6,100	VanCity - Segment B readvanceable	p+1
1,938	25,000	VanCity - unsecured C/L	P+1.5
$14,934			

$$\frac{\text{debit service}\ \ 14{,}934}{\text{income}\ \ 50{,}400} = 29.63\%$$

I look forward to hearing from you.

Yours truly,
SMITH CONSULTING GROUP LTD.

Fraser Smith
President

/leo
enclosure

Figure 6.1.2

mortgage. If the first is dropping at about $800 per month, the Whites want to ensure they invest the same amount by borrowing from their new investment line of credit. The interest expense on their new investment loan will be a tax deduction. The investment loan will increase at the same speed as the mortgage loan drops.

The Whites also cashed the liquid assets they owned, thus reducing their mortgage. Some of their GIC's will mature in the years ahead and will be applied against the mortgage. The pay downs will immediately be re-borrowed to invest. By June of this year (2002) the mortgage was down to $103,000.

It seems almost certain, based on their current progress, that the Whites should be finished with their bad debt mortgage in less than five years. Their debt should stay constant, good debt and bad debt combined, at around $155,000. The interest, in less than five years, should be totally deductible. At 7%, that would represent tax deductions in five years, of $10,850, every subsequent year that the Whites keep the deductible interest loan in place.

Because they very clearly understand the benefit of deductible versus non-deductible interest, the odds are very high that Brenda and Jim will still be collecting an annual tax deduction of $10,850 the year that they reach 130 years of age. Why would they ever use cash to pay off a tax-deductible loan? Better they should use that cash instead to pick up even more investments. Or maybe some of that cash could be used to increase their life style. Their choice.

Most banks, credit unions, trust companies and some life insurance companies have some variation on the readvanceable line of credit. Manulife has a very interesting product, which could be easily adopted to accommodate The Smith Manoeuvre. It is called *Manulife One*, and you can read about it at *www.manulifeone.com*. From the Home Page, select Mortgages and click on "what is Manulife One". You will also find a button called "Take The Challenge" which offers to pay appraisal and legal fees to switch. This financial offering looks excellent, and I predict that most institutions will have to offer similar programs as this instrument catches on. It is very popular in Australia.

If you are approaching your own bank to set you up for The Smith Manoeuvre, they may have enough information on hand to take care of you quickly.

If I were you, I would shop a bit, or use a financial planner to assist you. In that case, you will need the following information for the planner and the new banks you are approaching.

1. The usual questionnaire regarding address, phone, employer, years at current address, etc.
2. Proof of income. The income page from your tax returns or your recent pay stubs will do the trick.
3. A statement of net worth – assets and liabilities, which will indicate loans and payments.
4. You will likely need a recent statement regarding your current mortgage, and details regarding property tax. RRSP statements are an advantage.

The bank will do a credit check too. The fact that you are making arrangements to *convert* your debt as opposed to increasing it makes the decision easier for the bank. You are not asking to increase your credit, you are asking for rearrangements that will allow you to *convert* your credit. This will not be a hard decision for the banker in almost all cases. The fact that you already qualified for a mortgage somewhere else is great comfort to the banker who has a lot to gain by making you a new customer at the expenses of his competitor. So go get 'em!

Subsequent Account Adjustments

In the case of the Whites, you will notice on the first page of my proposal that if the house appraised at our estimate of $180,000, then there would be $6,100 available credit, for investment purposes. As it turned out, the house appraised at $184,000, so we re-submitted the adjusted proposal as follows:

	$184,000	appraised value
x .75	138,000	lending value – 75%
less	126,865	payout both BNS mortgages
	11,135	available credit

(I suggested to the Whites that they use some cash on hand to reduce the BNS second mortgage *prior* to calculating the three-month interest penalty for early payout, so the actual payout was less than the original proposal.)

Figure 6.3 is a copy of the VanCity Creditline Mortgage Agreement that shows at item number 1.4 that the Authorized Limit is $11,135.

Vancouver City Savings Credit Union
VICTORIA BRANCH
3055A SCOTT STREET, VICTORIA, B.C. V8 [illegible]
TELEPHONE 519-7000 / FAX 877-7042

June 7, 20001

KittyHawk Securities Ltd.
Attention: Fraser Smith

Re:
New First and Second Mortgages--.

Dear Fraser:

We are prepared to approve the following mortgage and unsecured creditline package:

1) Conventional First mortgage of +/- 75% of A.A.C.I. appraised value @ Prime + 0% (Homeprime) to payout and discharge the existing Bank of Nova Scotia first mortgage of +/- $88,900.00 and Bank of Nova Scotia Second mortgage of +/- $40,000.00 plus penalty. The payment will be based on a 25 yr. amortization.

2) Re-advanceable Second Mortgage Creditline mortgage up to 75% L.T.V., at Prime + 0% with payments to capitalize within the limit (Z1).

3) Unsecured $25,000.00 Creditline (Z2) at Prime plus 1.5% with interest payments to be paid monthly from the second mortgage creditline. Any loan interest due that exceeds authorized lending limits is to be paid by the borrowers on demand.

Please have the contact Bev at 519-7424 to book an appointment to sign our internal documents, prior to their appointment at Bob Adair's office to sign mortgage documents.

Yours truly,
Vancouver City Savings Credit Union

Greg Duncan
Manager

Figure 6.2

VanCity has agreed to lend a maximum of 75% of the appraised value of the prior mortgages. In this case, there is one prior VanCity mortgage of $126,865 (which used to be two prior mortgages at BNS). The rule VanCity will follow for the time being is that they will give the Whites an investment creditline of 75% of $184,000 *minus* $126,865 being the prior first mortgage amount at inception. The Authorized Limit of $11,135 is available now to borrow for investment purposes. The interest expense on the investment loan will be a tax deduction.

The first regular payment against the first mortgage will reduce the amount of the first mortgage principal. In addition, the Whites might take advantage of early payment provisions and make a lump sum reduction of the first mortgage. While the new equity generated is theoretically available to be re-borrowed, in practise, you will wait some months before you submit a request to recalculate a new, larger "Authorized Limit". The Whites would at least wait until they had nearly used up their investment creditline of $11,135.

To increase the "Authorized Limit", a written request is emailed to Greg Duncan or Bev Collison at VanCity requesting a readvance. VanCity confirms the current reduced amount of the first mortgage, subtracts that number from the 75% lending value, and the result is the new higher "Authorized Limit". If the first mortgage had gone down $5,000 since inception of the credit facility, then the "Authorized Limit" would increase by $5,000. This would allow the Whites several more months of investing at their predetermined rate of $800 per month.

When a readvance is approved, the Whites are asked to sign a new Creditline Mortgage Agreement for the higher amount.

The readvance process will continue every few months as needed, until the first mortgage has been paid off.

If the first mortgage were at a different institution, the Whites would need to obtain proof of the current first mortgage balance for VanCity's files.

And that's about it. Not so bad. It is a rather simple process actually, and it soon becomes a routine. But the magic of deductible interest is enhanced as each month goes by, and the results are predictable and exciting. It is truly worth the effort.

The Ten Steps of Implementation

Step 1 Find a banker who will agree to provide you Smith Manoeuvre facilities, subject to a written proposal from you or your financial planner and subject to an appraisal of the value of your home.

Step 2 Make a written proposal to the banker, built on the best guess you can make as to the value of your home, to be subsequently verified by an appraisal. You are requesting a readvanceable creditline, for 75% of the value of the appraisal, secured by a collateral mortgage on your home. Loan proceeds may be used to purchase investments.

Step 3 As soon as you are approved, subject to an appraisal, order the appraisal from a list of acceptable appraisers that the bank will provide to you.

Step 4 When the appraisal has been done, give it to the banker along with your revised proposal illustrating the adjusted request for your readvanceable creditline which will be for 75% of the appraised value of your home as indicated by the appraisal.

Step 5 When approval has been provided, the banker will recommend to you a lawyer, or perhaps you have one that is acceptable to the bank, where the new readvanceable creditline mortgage will be prepared for your signature.

Step 6 Get your new chequebook for your new investment creditline, and begin building an investment portfolio. As fast as you reduce the first mortgage, borrow back to invest.

Step 7 When your investment borrowings start to approach the "Authorized Limit" of your investment creditline, provide a written request to readvance the limit.

Step 8 Sell any paid up assets you may own such as term deposits, CSB's, GIC's, mutual funds, stocks, bonds, and real estate and apply the proceeds against your first mortgage. You may need your planner or accountant to calculate any capital gains triggered by the sale so you can determine your reserve for taxes. Readvance the investment creditline and re-borrow to replace tomorrow the assets you sold today. Use THE SMITHMAN CALCULATOR, (check box III), to see what this little move does for your future net worth. You will be surprised at the positive lift it provides to your net worth.

Step 9 Stop buying term deposits, CSB's, GIC's, mutual funds, stocks, bonds and real estate with your pay cheque. Instead, divert the funds you ordinarily would spend on these items, against your first mortgage. Then borrow the same amount of funds back again and purchase the intended investments with borrowed money.

Step 10 When you get your tax refund, be wise and pay this found money down against your first mortgage, then re-borrow the same amount and buy replacement investments.

You are on your way!

7

WHAT'S IN IT FOR THE BANK?

Life is Better When the Bank is Onside

Canadians, like people everywhere, love to hate the banks. Canadians are reasonable though - they don't play favourites. They hate all banks equally. The bank is the lightening rod for all things negative in our financial lives. Things have been going badly for most Canadians these past few years as we lose more and more purchasing power each year. It is no secret that our standard of living in Canada has been dropping year by year for some time now.

The blame for our national despair should more properly be laid at the feet of the elected dictatorship that is our government. The financial erosion we are experiencing has evolved in part because of the arrogance, debt, mismanagement, waste and corruption of the past few Liberal and Conservative governments.

But the banks deserve a share of the blame. They have been quick to raise service fees for reduced services while turning in record profits, which is galling to most Canadians. So the banks are not blameless. When you are having trouble making ends meet for your family, it stings that the president of the bank who holds your mortgage earned over five million dollars in salary alone last year. There is something wrong with this picture.

In the meantime, we must work with the hand we've been dealt. We may resent the banks, but any mortgage strategy that is going to be good for your financial well being will have to benefit the powerful banks as well, or you can bet it won't be happening. Fortunately or unfortunately, The Smith Manoeuvre will make even more money for the banks, right from the get-go, so they won't mind co-operating with you when you approach them to help you establish it.

If your mortgage is at a big bank, you might want to consider taking your Smith Manoeuvre business to a credit union. These are the little guys fighting the giant banks for market share, and we need credit unions for the minor amount of competition that they bring to bear on the big banks. Every little bit of competition for the big banks defers a tiny bit the day they will control everything and everybody. You can make a difference.

The Smith Manoeuvre can be established for you at your current bank that holds your first mortgage, or at any other bank or credit union. The bank that does The Smith Manoeuvre for you will be working around your first mortgage whether they have it already, or whether it is at some other institution. Other than the convenience of perhaps having all your banking at one facility, it will make little difference to you personally. If you have time and patience, you might shop around to find out which institution really wants your business enough to give you some perks for bringing The Smith Manoeuvre to them.

Way Back Then

When I was first attempting to interest a bank to support my invention in 1984, I was turned down by the Royal, the Montreal and the Bank of BC in that order. "Irregular" was the common reason given for refusing to participate to bring tax relief to Canadian mortgage holders.

Not one to give up, I decided I needed to talk to a bank president. Guessing that I would not be getting an audience any time soon with the president of the Royal Bank, I elected instead to talk to the president of VanCity Savings. The Chief Executive Officer was Larry Bell, recently arrived from his tenure as Deputy Minister of Finance for British Columbia. The VanCity board had decided they wanted to make things happen, and they couldn't have picked a better man for the job. I didn't know Larry Bell from a stick, but when I placed my call, the operator put me through without asking my name, and Larry Bell answered the phone himself. I liked him immediately. I told him I had an idea that would bring VanCity new customers at the expense of the big banks and he invited me in for a visit the following week.

Larry listened intently to my story, watched me draw my little pictorial, and when I was finished, he asked, "why isn't every Canadian doing this?" And a friendship was born.

Larry had his managers, corporate lawyers and senior staff review my proposal for comment. He took it to the board for their blessing, and within two months I began making mortgages deductible for the families in my client base. Larry

Bell went on to be chairman of BC Hydro. Following a couple of other assignments he is back as chairman of BC Hydro once again, at the request of the BC government.

Larry was a finance MBA, not a banker, and some would say that is the only reason he would even consider giving me and my Manoeuvre a chance. I think that is part of it, but I also think it is because he is a gentleman, and a gentle man, who saw potential where others didn't. What Larry allowed me to do for my clients, he is now doing for you because without his foresight and his intuition, I would probably not be writing this book for you today.

VanCity has grown to be the largest credit union in Canada. I am told that in the entire world, only the Boeing Credit Union is larger. VanCity continues to win prizes as one of the best companies to work for in Canada. It is home to Tom Hancock, the best banker I ever met. Tom was the branch manager of the North Vancouver branch of VanCity when we got The Smith Manoeuvre under way back in 1984. Tom is still with VanCity, and if you're lucky enough to live in B.C.'s Lower Mainland, you don't need to read this book any further. Just call Tom at (604) 877-7180. You can also call Diana Lingholt, the other best banker I ever met, (604) 877-7161. Diana knows The Smith Manoeuvre inside out. VanCity's Victoria experts are Greg Duncan and Bev Collison, 519-7425, or toll free 1-866-323-8383.

What was it that interested Larry Bell?

There are several reasons that Larry Bell was interested in The Smith Manoeuvre for VanCity's benefit.

1. Client profile

My client profile included presidents, managers, business people and lots of ordinary people too. At that time, having come from servicing largely the blue-collar sector, it was interesting to VanCity that they could perhaps attract other sectors too.

(Any financial planner reading this book should consider contacting every client immediately to offer an introduction to a credit union that will assist them with The Smith Manoeuvre. Every credit union manager should contact every customer to offer The Smith Manoeuvre before some other bank or credit union does the same.)

2. New customers

Since everybody already has a banking relationship, it is a market that is nearly 100% saturated. You may not feel sorry for your bank manager, but he is measured on how many new customers he signs up in the branch each year. As in most businesses, they need new business to grow, but that's tough to do in the banking business. By co-operating with me, the credit union attracted customers from other banks, other trust companies and other credit unions who were not offering The Smith Manoeuvre.

The bulk of my client base became VanCity customers. Why wouldn't they? VanCity allowed them to make their mortgage tax deductible, and their bank did not.

3. Good customers

By virtue of the nature of the loan set-up I was proposing, Larry could see that his loan risk was very modest. This was partly because his security for the investment lending would be the house, not the investments the client would be purchasing. I am sure Larry was very confident that you would make fantastic investments with the money he was going to be lending you, but just in case, he would rather have your house as security for his loan to you. You are indifferent because you have already given your house as collateral to the Royal Bank, say, where you have your first mortgage. Does it matter to you if the two banks are willing to share the same collateral security for their respective loans?

The main reason the loan risk was low was because Larry would not be lending to my client unless my client had first reduced the debt on his first mortgage. Accordingly, Larry's lending was not increasing the customer's debt; it was simply keeping it at the same level. Down goes the mortgage at the Royal; up goes the investment loan at VanCity.

Assuming that Larry would not accept my client if he did not have a good payment record on his existing first mortgage at the Royal, it would be a fairly safe bet that my client would not default at VanCity. In other words, the Royal has already spent the time and money to qualify the customer for a mortgage, which reduces the risk to VanCity.

And to this day, no client on The Smith Manoeuvre has ever defaulted. It is a fact that in all the years since 1984 that The Smith Manoeuvre has been operated by VanCity or any other credit union, not one mortgage loan, nor one investment loan has gone bad. It is also a fact that no bank or credit union that has utilized The Smith Manoeuvre has ever lost a penny of interest or principal to any client of mine. The Smith Manoeuvre business has been gold plated for VanCity and Coast Capital. You will know that all banks and credit unions expect and plan to have some mortgages and loans that fail, so it is a strong testament to The Smith Manoeuvre that the record is pristine.

4. Collateral business

The new VanCity customer represented by my client seeking support to do The Smith Manoeuvre was bringing new lending business for VanCity. My proposal was that VanCity lend to my client every dollar that my client paid off against his first mortgage at the Royal. The security for this new loan for investment purposes would be the same house that was security for the first mortgage at the Royal.

In addition to their regular mortgage payments at the original bank, my clients were encouraged to make additional reductions against their first mortgage. VanCity would then lend back the amount that had been paid down on the first, and the new borrowings at VanCity would buy investments, thus the interest would be tax deductible. The faster my clients reduced their first mortgage, the faster they were able to borrow back the same amount, to be invested. The tax deductions got larger. They were applied against the first mortgage too, as additional pay downs. As soon as the first mortgage dropped, VanCity lent it back to my client again, and around we would go again. The first mortgage melted away, the investment loan at VanCity grew at exactly the same speed, no faster. More tax deductions, more first mortgage reductions, more borrowing from VanCity to invest, more tax deductions.

There is a giant sucking sound as VanCity starts to pull the 25-year asset, your mortgage, from the safe at the Royal Bank and puts it into their vaults. The little guy has swiped the Royal's asset before they even know it has gone. The Royal was planning on you sweating and grunting for the next 25 years on their behalf so they could make huge sums of interest (non-deductible interest) on your back. Suddenly the asset has disappeared, an exceedingly troubling development because mortgage lending is a huge profit centre to the banks.

It's true that VanCity will be charging you interest as well. But there is a huge and fantastic difference. *The interest you pay at VanCity is tax deductible.* It never was deductible at the Royal. In addition to that, in making the conversion from non-deductible to deductible debt, you have built a large investment portfolio. Best of all, the investments are free and clear. No margin calls. VanCity did not take your investments as collateral because you gave VanCity the security of the same house that you had given the Royal. The Royal won't be needing the collateral anymore because they don't have your mortgage debt anymore. Their asset has evaporated to the nether regions.

Remember, the mortgage loan is your liability, therefore the bank's asset. Mortgage assets are the bank's lifeblood. They need as many mortgages as they can find. By allowing you to implement The Smith Manoeuvre, VanCity has found a way to obtain new mortgage assets by stealing them away from the big banks in exchange for giving you some unique and original investment financing, at no cost to VanCity. Once you are their happy customer they will be in a position to offer you legal services, RRSP/RRIF services, mutual funds, securities, trust services and insurance services. You are an important asset to any bank or credit union that is lucky enough to call you their customer.

There are Other Benefits for the Lending Institution

5. They don't have to pay for the benefit you receive.

The banks will be pleased, nay anxious, to show you how to profit through The Smith Manoeuvre. After all, it is the tax department that is giving you this extraordinary financial benefit, not the banks, so why wouldn't they be pleased to profit by showing you the way to engineer these free tax refunds?

6. Low up-front cost to the banks.

The front-end costs to the bank in order to receive large benefits such as 25 years of mortgage interest from the sweat of your brow are small.

Usually when the banks offer you incentives to switch your mortgage to them, they pay a stiff up-front price. 5% cash back, free appraisal, and free legals, front-end interest rate discounts – these are expensive methods for the banks to utilize to convince you to switch. They do it because they need more and more new business in order to grow, just like any other business. That they will absorb these punishing up front costs in order to get you to place your mortgage with them is testament to the huge value the mortgage business represents to the lending institutions.

The banks will be delighted to provide you the new Smith Manoeuvre Mortgage because it will cost them very little to give you the financial arrangements required to put the strategy in place.

7. The banks will sell you the investments you need to make the program work.

Elsewhere in this book I have described the monopoly position that the banks are quickly approaching regarding everything financial in the lives of Canadians. I regret to say that there is another advantage for the banks when they begin providing The Smith Manoeuvre offerings to you.

Because my strategy does not work if you don't borrow funds to invest (in order to bring in new money via tax deductions) you will find yourself borrowing to invest. This is fine for you because it makes the program work and you will be grateful to have an investment portfolio that grows rapidly.

The banks, however, have also gotten into the investment business. They will rush to facilitate The Smith Manoeuvre for you because their costs to do so are light, and because the benefits you receive are at the expense of the tax department. They will also want to sell you the investments you need to buy in order to get the tax deductions. This may well be the biggest of all the advantages for the lending institutions – they get first crack at selling investments to the family to whom they just did the favour of rearranging their financing so that the family could implement The Smith Manoeuvre. What a lovely business position to be in.

The minute this book is on the shelves, if I were a bank, I would be working 25 hours a day to ensure that when you walk in to ask that The Smith Manoeuvre be set up for you, I will be ready to supply your investments as well as your financing.

What will your revised bank statement look like?

It's really very simple to do. As your banker, I would offer you a monthly bank statement that showed how much your first mortgage went down in the last 30 days whether by regular mortgage payments or over payments (look at the Manulife One Program for a slick way to do this. *www.manulifeone.com*). On the same page I would show you that the exact amount of the mortgage reduction had been loaned back to you to buy the three or six mutual funds that you chose when you signed up for The Smith Manoeuvre.

Your statement would show:

a. how much your mortgage dropped that month
b. that the same amount was loaned back to you the same day from a separate creditline (tracking is important)
c. which investments were purchased with the borrowed money
d. how much interest was charged on the investment loan so that you can see how much your tax deduction increased that month

e. your total deductible interest accumulated year to date
f. what the total value of your investments were standing at from inception to date. This investment pool is completely liquid and is free and clear because your house is the security for the borrowings, not the investments.

If you feel strongly that the banks already have too much power over you, then why not consider starting at the credit union when you do your research. You may find that their services are better than these at the banks. You will also feel good you are supporting competition to the monster banks. Your financial planner will help you choose a financial institution that will offer the services you need to optimize your tax deductions using The Smith Manoeuvre.

8. Self maintaining asset base

It was Larry Bell who pointed out to me one of the most important benefits he could see accruing to VanCity.

All banks have a built in problem with their mortgage loan assets. The day you made your first mortgage payment, you reduced your principal a tiny amount, in addition to paying a huge amount of non-deductible interest to the bank. While you feel good about paying down your mortgage balance, the bank feels bad, because you have reduced their asset. They start immediately to find other people who need mortgages in order to replace the assets lost each day due to mortgage payments being made across Canada.

It was Larry who realized that because my clients would be re-borrowing to invest at the same speed as they were paying off the first mortgage, the consequence would be that his bank's asset, your debt, would be maintained at the same level. Why would you pay off a loan you had just made deductible?

Why indeed! Your intent should be to die at age 130 still owing VanCity that same amount so that you can keep claiming the deductible interest every year until you die.

Assume that after a few years, the whole mortgage has been converted to the deductible interest investment loan. Assume you keep the deductible loan going, so that you would have the same tax deductions year after year.

These annual, repeating, large, free, no-cost, gratis and non-taxable annual tax refunds would be pooled with the former first mortgage payment which you don't need to make anymore because the conversion is complete.

In practice, you would reduce your newly converted investment loan with the total of the tax refunds and the former first mortgage payment, but just for a day. The rule is that if you reduce your creditline, you can borrow the money back, less the interest expense (tax-deductible) for that month. You would borrow back the difference and invest it. You would continue each month to build your investment portfolio at the maximum rate, the tax deductions would be maximum, and the deductible loan would stay constantly level as you paid interest only, on the loan. The interest expense would continue to be deductible every year for the rest of your life and your investment portfolio would continue to grow as you added more capital each month. If your income was a bit low when you retired, you might slow down or cease to add capital into your investment portfolio. If it were still too low, perhaps you would set up a SWP, or Systematic Withdrawal Plan such that the investment portfolio started sending you a cheque each month, for a change.

If you complete the conversion, and wish to have no debt at all, good or bad, you could elect to divert tax refunds plus former first mortgage payments to reduce the deductible loan. The price of no debt would be tax deductions that would get smaller each year as the deductible loan was reduced. As well, if your excess cash flow is being diverted to pay off this good loan, by definition, your excess cash flow is not building a larger investment portfolio, to the detriment of your retirement planning.

The point is that you will have a choice between continuing your investment program or paying off your new tax-deductible loan. This is a luxury many Canadians will not enjoy if they do not avail themselves of at least employing The Smith Manoeuvre to convert the debt from the bad kind to the good kind. Convert your debt to the good kind, and then decide whether to keep it or pay it off.

That is the very least even the most debt-adverse citizen should entertain. If you already have the debt of a first mortgage, at least convert it from bad debt to good debt. The benefits are large:

1. It costs you nothing, but for the appraisal and the cost of the mortgage documents, which many lending institutions will absorb if you simply ask, (they need mortgage business with low risk customers and it costs them very little both to verify the value of your house and to prepare a re-advanceable mortgage using in-house or related specialists).

2. You will reduce your first mortgage with tax deductions that are free for the asking.

3. You will have an investment portfolio that will grow year after year contributing income into your retirement – an investment portfolio that, otherwise, you would not have had.

4. If your investment program is made up of financial assets such as mutual funds, stocks and bonds, you will have complete liquidity if for any reason you need to reverse the program.

You will be pleased when you decide to utilize The Smith Manoeuvre. The financial institutions will also be glad of your decision. But will the tax department be glad you did? Will the Minister of Revenue be excited in a pleasant and positive way when you have engineered all these continuous and very large tax deductions year after year after year? Hmmm-mm.

Just who is providing all this new money you are getting from all these new tax deductions you are claiming for your new found deductible interest?

8

WHAT'S IN IT FOR CANADA?

The Tax Department, the Government and the Country

There is a rumour that the tax department is planning a new tax return for Canadians. They have been listening to citizens who think its format should be a simpler form, and this is the first draft:

1. How much did you make last year?
2. Send it in.

Who Pays?

Just where is all this new money coming from that your family is going to receive in order for you to utilize The Smith Manoeuvre, *so that you can:*

1. reduce your first mortgage, *so that you can*

2. borrow back your new found equity the same day, *so that you can*
3. buy new investments with the new, borrowed money, *so that you can*
4. generate deductible investment-loan interest expense, *so that you can*
5. claim tax deductions, *so that you can*
6. get free tax refund cheques, *so that you can*

1. reduce your first mortgage, *so that you can*
2. borrow back,........etc., etc.

It becomes apparent that *the tax department is the entity that is going to provide the new money for your family* when you engage The Smith Manoeuvre. There are many articles and books written that show you how to pay your mortgage off faster, and this is good because it means you will pay less interest to the bank over the life of the mortgage.

But it is important to understand that these strategies, such as switching from monthly mortgage payments to making payments every two weeks, are only effective because you are putting *more of your own money* against the mortgage sooner. It is the "sooner" part that shortens the life of the mortgage, thus reducing the total amount of interest that you will pay. While that's good, it is still *your money* that is being *spent sooner*. The payoff for you comes at the back end of the mortgage, which is many years off. Would you be interested in having your payoff start right now?

The Smith Manoeuvre is quite different because it is the only mortgage strategy that generates a new and incremental income for your family via tax deductions, which you are then able to use to pay down your mortgage faster than otherwise possible. In addition, you will have a pool of assets you have purchased with the money you borrowed to invest - all because you receive new cash for your family as a result of tax refund cheques that you receive from the tax department. This should make you feel better towards the tax department.

Because this investment strategy converts the traditionally non-deductible interest of a house mortgage loan into deductible investment-loan interest, the tax department will not be receiving as much tax from you as they have become accustomed to receiving. They will still be collecting a lot from you, but less than usual.

In the narrow confines of the office of the Minister of Revenue, there might be some early consternation at the initial drop in tax revenue because of the refund cheques he will be writing to you when you start using The Smith Manoeuvre. Fortunately, the Minister of Revenue, in the longer term, is quite happy to have you using The Smith Manoeuvre.

Deductible Interest – the Lubricant of Business Investment

Most industrialized nations allow the interest expense on business loans to be deducted from the business income of the corporation that does the borrowing. This act reduces the income tax bill of the company. The government understands quite well that it is in their own best interest to provide the tax incentive of tax-deductible interest to businesses making investment decisions for the benefit of their own company. For instance, if the loan interest is deductible, then it makes more palatable the decision to build plant and infrastructure.

The taxman knows that if he does his part to make it easier for the companies to make decisions to borrow to invest in infrastructure, research, marketing and such, there will likely be more profits in the future for the company which the taxman will be able to tax. In addition, the growth of the company will require growth in the number of employed people who the tax department will be only too happy to tax to the max.

This also reduces the number of people on the welfare rolls, reducing government expense in that important area. The people who are working ostensibly spend more providing a stimulus to the economy, further increasing the flows of cash which government also gets to tax to death. You are familiar with the GST, no doubt.

And finally, whereas people who are without work are a drain on the system on a current basis, they are also not investors in RRSP's and other investments, which would provide future income for their retirement. The government gains in a large way if the population is employed. These are some of the reasons that the tax department is happy to allow deductible interest for businesses that borrow to increase their business. And so it should be.

Personal Investing and Tax Deductible Interest

The wealthier of the population, after the expenses we all have for food, clothing, shelter and income tax, have some money left over at the end of the month to invest. They are also able to afford expensive lawyers and accountants to show them how to take out bank loans for investment purposes and then to deduct their interest on their investment loans, simultaneously. Invest and also reduce income tax at the same time? That's fine by the tax department, and is in fact encouraged by the tax department. All wealthy people have done this, are doing it or will do it.

Because the wealthy are able and willing to invest to improve their economic position to even higher levels, they provide the rest of us a service of great benefit. Because of their investment money, new businesses are funded, and the new businesses hire new people. The businesses and the people are taxed, so the taxman is grateful enough to the investor that the taxman will allow the wealthy investor to deduct the interest on any loan he takes out for the purpose of earning more income. The rationale is the same as it is for the first example of the taxman allowing deductions of interest expense for companies.

The 90% or more of the population that are not classified as wealthy are not usually investors. It is not because they don't want to be, it's because they usually find that the cash runs out before the month runs out. How could anyone justify using cash to invest for say a 10% return when they are carrying credit card debt at 19%? We know that only 1 in 3 Canadians can afford to invest in an RRSP even with its great benefits such as tax deductibility of the principal investment plus tax-free compounding. Small wonder that by far the bulk of Canadians will come up short of cash flow when the pay cheque stops at retirement day.

The Smith Manoeuvre works for all Canadians who have a mortgage, whether they are wealthy or not. There is a huge pool of mortgage payers in Canada that are not in the wealthy category. They are working hard to make ends meet, they are getting an education, and they are raising kids. They are also finding it tough to get through many months without employing the credit card.

The tax department will be delighted to find out that The Smith Manoeuvre is going to turn this huge group of taxpayers into investors. More investors in Canada means more businesses funded with new funds as the mortgages are converted from dead-end home mortgages into investment loans.

The benefits for Canada will be the same as they are from companies that invest, and from wealthy Canadians that invest. And therefore, in the same way the tax department is happy to allow deductions for interest on loans to make income when it applies to business and wealthy investors, they will be happy to allow it for the not-so-wealthy. If you are in the not-so-wealthy category, the tax department is standing by to start sending you tax refund cheques if you are wise enough to convert your bad debt to good debt.

Because of the resultant new cash that will begin arriving in the homes of legions of ordinary Canadians derived from these tax refund cheques, these families will be better off themselves. They will have pools of investments instead of dead-end house mortgages, and they will generate lower and lower taxes as they invest more and more. These families will be less likely to need government assistance during their working life or in their retirement.

The tax department is the apparent loser in the short term, but a winner in the longer term. This is why the government, in its wisdom, will bless The Smith Manoeuvre and the wealth it will bring to homeowners with mortgages, be they wealthy or not-so-wealthy.

A decade ago, Joe Clark was elected prime minister partly on the strength of his promise to give Canadians tax-deductible mortgages. To his credit, the law was changed and the tax return forms the following year did provide some partial deductions. The Liberals cancelled the program when Joe was defeated at the next election. The flaw in the program was that it was a giveaway. There was no requirement for the homeowner to do any investing/conversion of the mortgage to earn the deductions. You will receive no tax refunds from the taxman using The Smith Manoeuvre unless and until you convert your debt from bad to good. Investing is good for the people, and therefore it's good for Canada. In the final analysis, this is why the CCRA will be happy to support The Smith Manoeuvre, and this is why you will receive free tax refunds.

It will sound to some like it is too good to be true, that life is a zero sum game and therefore it can't possibly be as represented. Classical and modern economists might not agree on the foregoing as it applies to theory. But if you believe in free enterprise and the goodness of capitalism-with-caring, you will understand that we can all be beneficiaries if we enable and encourage this program. The Smith Manoeuvre simply extends tax and investment benefits that have always been in place for business and the wealthy, to the less wealthy in our society. Surely that will be good for all of us.

9

SUMMARY

You have learned about The Smith Manoeuvre, which is a combination of several different strategies available to you that, once implemented, will improve the financial well being of your family in dramatic fashion, with very little cost.

These strategies rapidly convert bad debt (non-deductible) to good debt (tax deductible) and they work on any current or future non-deductible interest debt you may have, including house mortgages, car loans and consolidation loans.

The Smith Manoeuvre *does not require* that you increase your debt. Instead you will simply arrange to keep the amount of your existing debt constant for the interval of time it takes to *convert* the debt you have now, from the bad kind to the good kind.

When the conversion process has been completed, you may choose to resume eliminating your debt, even though it is good debt (the interest expense is tax deductible and will be providing you free tax refund cheques).

In the alternative, you may decide that you wish to leave the loan in place, paying deductible interest only. In this case you will continue to receive tax refund cheques, and instead of reducing the loan with your cash flow, you could choose to continue to buy investments. The decision is yours to make, at your pleasure.

The length of time it will take to convert your existing bad debt to good debt is influenced by several factors. These include your family cash flow, the amount of deductible interest you can claim to get tax refunds, and the value of assets you currently own. These assets might better be liquidated to provide more cash to reduce your non-deductible loans such as your house mortgage. In addition, the efficiency of The Smith Manoeuvre can be dramatically improved by diverting existing monthly savings and investment plans against the non-deductible debt.

As the non-deductible loans are reduced by the foregoing strategies, the identical amount of money is re-borrowed from the same or a different bank to purchase replacement assets. These assets will be free and clear because the security for the borrowing will be the house, just as the house was the security for the original non-deductible mortgage loan.

Because these new assets are free and clear, there can be no margin calls. If your family were subsequently subjected to a financial disaster, such that your house was in danger, you would obviously sell off some of your free and clear assets to ensure you kept your home.

The Smith Manoeuvre relies on the tax department rules that money borrowed to buy your home, cars, vacations and consolidation, does not generate deductible interest. On the other hand, when you borrow money with the expectation of earning more income, the interest expense of that loan *will* be a tax deduction. It is the kind of debt you have that determines its deductibility.

You have the debt already. It is bad debt because its interest expense is not tax deductible. You might as well get it converted to the good kind of debt – deductible debt. You will enjoy receiving those tax refund cheques. They are free and there is no tax on the proceeds. The conversion from bad debt to good debt is effected by your purchase of new investments of your choice, one more very large benefit of The Smith Manoeuvre for your family.

The Smith Manoeuvre is a legal strategy utilizing standard Canada Customs and Revenue Agency tax rules. It is available to any Canadian family with 25% or more equity in their home, or with the ability to engineer 25% or more equity by paying down or borrowing enough to reach that level. Borrowing from Peter to pay Paul is not always a bad thing to do.

The Smith Manoeuvre utilizes strategies routinely practised by businesses and wealthy individuals with the assistance of expensive lawyers and accountants. Finally, via The Smith Manoeuvre, ordinary Canadians with ordinary incomes will be able to enjoy these strategies previously available only to the wealthy.

To enable you to calculate your personal outcomes if you were to employ The Smith Manoeuvre for your family, you will want to order THE SMITHMAN CALCULATOR at *www.smithman.net*, or photocopy the order form on the last page of this book to send in. This versatile software will show you the results arising from any partial or complete implementation of the program. It will allow you to compare "what-if" strategies such as interest rate variations or amortization alterations. You will be able to compare the performance results of The Smith

Manoeuvre versus the David Chilton wealth creation method and the Garth Turner strategy as well.

The financial course currently being travelled by most Canadians these days will yield poor results and broken dreams. Adopting The Smith Manoeuvre will dramatically improve your chances of optimizing your ability to build significantly more family net worth than you presumed possible.

While it is possible for a person with some financial experience to put The Smith Manoeuvre into practice, I recommend you employ a financial planner to do this work for you. A full service financial planner will be able to tailor your financial situation to your best personal advantage. There are also other circumstances and linkages that a good financial planner will accommodate on your behalf to ensure no opportunity is missed to optimize the results for your family. Go to my website *www.smithman.net* to get assistance in locating a financial planner in your part of Canada, who is qualified to assist you with implementation of The Smith Manoeuvre or check Appendix A.1.

Factors that influence the financial well being of your family have not been encouraging in

Canada in the past few years, and a turn around may be slower coming than we would hope. This means we will have to depend less on government, and more on our own resources. The Smith Manoeuvre is remarkably efficient at raising large amounts of real, new money for your family while it generates welcome and free tax refunds. As well, it causes us to immediately begin building that all-important investment portfolio that will give us peace of mind as it builds, free and clear. It is a comfort to live your life knowing you have liquid assets to call upon if the need ever arises.

So join the hundreds of Canadians who are already in the process of converting their bad debt to good debt, or who have completed the process. You too can enjoy these financial gains for the benefit of your family.

I

APPENDICES

EXPERIENCED FINANCIAL PLANNERS

Unless you have financial planning experience, I recommend you locate a financial planner in your area who is interested in assisting with the implementation of *The Smith Manoeuvre* for you. A few minutes on the telephone to find someone who is willing to help will be very worthwhile.

On the website www.smithman.net is a button called "Find A Planner" where we are listing financial planners who are willing to assist with *The Smith Manoeuvre*, for a fee. Most will be happy to make your first meeting complimentary, but do inquire.

If you are a financial planner, and if you would be willing to assist mortgage owners with this strategy, please fax your request on your letterhead to (250) 652-0835. There is no charge for this listing, but I do require that you have a financial designation. We are pleased to include any education designation you may have as well.

FINANCIAL DESIGNATIONS

A.I.C.B.	Associate of the Institute of Canadian Bankers
A.C.F.P.	Associate Certificate in Financial Planning
Adm.A.Pl.Fin.	Adminstrateure agréé en planification financière
AFC	Accredited Financial Counsellor
CA	Chartered Accountant
C.Adm. F.P.	Chartered Administrator in Financial Planning
CAM	Certified Administrative Manager
Cert.Bus.Admin.	Certificate in Business Administration
CFA	Chartered Financial Analyst
CFP	Chartered Financial Planner
CFP	Certified Financial Planner
C.G.A.	Certified General Accountant
CH.F.C.	Chartered Financial Consultant
CIM	Certified Investment Manager
CLU	Chartered Life Underwriter
C.M.A.	Certified Management Accountant
CMC	Certified Management Consultant
Dipl.Bus.Admin.	Diploma Business Administration
FCA	Fellow Chartered Accountant
FCI	Fellow of the Credit Institute

F.C.I.A.	Fellow of the Canadian Institute of Actuaries
FCSI	Fellow of the Canadian Securities Institute
FIIC	Fellow of the Insurance Institute of Canada
M.T.C.I.	Member of Trust Companies Institute
MTI	Member of the Trust Institute
P.F.C.	Planificateure Financier Certifié
PRP	Professional Retirement Planner
R.F.P.	Registered Financial Planner

BRIAN DOUGHERTY LTD.
CHARTERED ACCOUNTANTS

202 - 315 WEST 1st STREET
NORTH VANCOUVER, B.C. V7M 1B5
TELEPHONE: (604) 986-7307
FAX: (604) 984-6919
E-MAIL: brian@briandougherty.com

June 24, 2002

Smith Consulting Group Ltd.
104 – 7851 East Saanich Road
Saanichton, BC
V8M 2B4

Dear Sirs:

Re: Review of Excel Model Titled The Smith Manoeuvre

We have conducted a review of the Excel spreadsheet entitled The Smith Manoeuvre version Model 6 with a view to confirming it's basic mathematical assumptions, mechanics of operation and subsequent results.

Amortization results using Model 6 with several different variables as to rates and amortization periods were compared against Mortgage 2 Pro for Windows software, version 4.05.004, and the results were precisely the same in all tests we preformed. The interest compounding variables of Model 6 are limited to two interest compounding methodologies, standard Canadian mortgage compounding which is twice yearly, not in advance, and standard monthly compounding which covers American mortgages and standard loan amortization in both countries.

-2-

Model 6 includes a standard amortization calculator as well as a modified amortization calculator which allows the user to quickly compare the effects of making additional payments against mortgages and loans in order to reduce the total interest expense of those mortgages and loans. In addition to the foregoing, Model 6 supplies additional capability to extrapolate the conversion of the interest saved into additional investments over the same periods of time represented by the original amortization expectations of the original loan.

The net result is that Model 6 is able to show the favourable effect of converting the non-deductible interest of the house mortgage into the deductible interest of an equivalent investment loan which in turn, generates tax refunds for the user.

We have checked the assumptions and mechanics of these sections of Model 6 and we confirm that the assumptions are acceptable and the calculated results are as would be expected.

Yours very truly,

Brian Dougherty Ltd.
Chartered Accountants

Per: Brian Dougherty

/blc

II

LINKS

Websites

The Smith Manoeuvre	*www.smithman.net*
Canadian Assoc. of Financial Planners	*www.cafp.org*
Garth Turner	*www.garth.ca*
The Fraser Institute	*www.fraserinstitute.ca*
Andex Charts	*www.andexcharts.com*
Talbot Stevens	*www.talbotstevens.com*
Manulife	*www.manulifeone.com*
Canadian Taxpayers Federation	*www.taxpayer.com*
National Citizens Coalition	*www.morefreedom.org*
VanCity Savings Credit Union	*www.vancity.com*
Coast Capital Savings	*www.coastcapitalsavings.com*
Amortization.com	*www.morgij2.com*

III

WHAT PEOPLE ARE SAYING...

"I would like to tell you that I introduced your strategy to my financial planner and he was very excited about it. He said he'd start to offer this strategy to other clients. Again thank you for the great idea."
Mark Libant, Ottawa, Ont. March 2003

"Fraser Smith's door ought to have been knocked down hundreds of times. It ought to have been torn from its hinges and thrust aside as mortgage-weary Canadians stormed in to see the man who could help them pay down that mortgage faster and write off the interest like their American cousins."
"Financial Planner Manoeuvres Rules and Banks to Your Benefit"
Andrew Duffy, Times Colonist, January 22, 2003

"A must read for those looking to reduce their tax bill and increase their financial security."
Canadian Taxpayers Federation
The Taxpayer, December 2002/January 2003 issue

"You're converting mortgage interest into a 100-per-cent tax deduction, year after year, which will garner you nice fat tax refunds."
B.C. Business "Home Leverage" – December 2002

"...a snowballing virtuous circle that lets you tweak the noses of both the banks and the taxman."
Johnathan Chevreau
National Post – December 19, 2002

ORDER FORM
SMITH CONSULTING GROUP LTD.

NEED GIFTS FOR FRIENDS AND FAMILY WITH MORTGAGES?

Qty	DESCRIPTON	Each	TOTAL	
	THE SMITHMAN CALCULATOR CD Software	$39.95		
	THE SMITH MANOEUVRE Book	$24.95		
1	Shipping and Handling	$ 9	9	00
		Subtotal		
	(GST #13597 49620)	7% GST		
	(B.C. residents, software only)	7.5% PST		
		TOTAL		

Call toll-free for discount rates for 11 or more CD's, or 11 or more books. **1-800-792-0825**

☐ Cheque, draft or money order for $_________ Canadian, payable to **SCGL** (Smith Consulting Group Ltd.)

☐ Please charge $__________________ Canadian to my card:
O VISA O MasterCard O AMEX

Card number: ______________________________ Expiry:______
Name on Card:_______________________________________
Signature: ____

YOU
Apt: _______________
Address: ____
City/Town: ___________________________Prov: ________
Postal Code: _______________ Phone: (____)______________
Email: ____

US
Order by Fax: (250) 652-0835
Order by Mail: The Smith Manoeuvre
Box 42,
Saanichton, B.C. V8M 2C3
Order by Internet: *www.smithman.net*
Order by Toll Free Phone: 1-800-792-0825

V

37% DISCOUNT COUPON

Now that you have read the book, you will want to order "THE SMITHMAN CALCULATOR". This CD provides a unique program that will allow you to forecast the advantages that will come to your family if you implement *The Smith Manoeuvre*. Using your own mortgage assumptions, the CD will project and graph your debt, your tax deductions, your tax refunds and your portfolio values over the next 25 years.

The CD ordinarily sells for $39.95 plus taxes and shipping and handling. This Discount Coupon provides a 37.5% discount of $15 to reduce the price of the CD to $24.95 plus taxes and shipping and handling.

Simply mail this coupon with your cheque made payable to SCGL for $24.95 + $5.00 (s/h) plus $2.10 GST (total of $32.05) to SCGL, P.O. Box 42, Saanichton, B.C. V8M 2C3.

If you prefer, call toll free 1-800-792-0825 and order with your credit card.

For additional information, including computer system requirements, visit our website, www.smithman.net.

ISBN 155369641-7
9 781553 696414